ULTIMATE GUIDE TO
TAE KWON DO

Edited by
John R. Little and Curtis F. Wong

CONTEMPORARY BOOKS

Library of Congress Cataloging-in-Publication Data

Cover design by Todd Petersen
Cover and interior photographs courtesy of CFW Enterprises
Interior design by Amy Yu Ng

Published by Contemporary Books
A division of NTC/Contemporary Publishing Group, Inc.
4255 West Touhy Avenue, Lincolnwood (Chicago), Illinois 60712-1975 U.S.A.
Copyright © 2000 by John R. Little and Curtis F. Wong
Printed in the United States of America
International Standard Book Number: 0-8092-2831-9

  00 01 02 03 04 VL 18 17 16 15 14 13 12 11 10 9 8 7 6 5 4 3 2

Ultimate Guide to
TAE KWON DO

Contents

PART III: TECHNIQUES

Preface

Tae Kwon Do is without question the most popular martial art in North America today. With *dojangs* (training halls) on almost every corner, you probably know somebody who is presently studying the art. For more than twenty-five years, CFW Enterprises, through its publications *Inside Kung Fu, Inside Karate,* and, of course, *Inside Tae Kwon Do,* has been in the vanguard of promoting Tae Kwon Do, advancing this art by bringing its background, training methods, and techniques to the attention of Tae Kwon Doists the world over.

Within the pages of this book you will be treated to a cornucopia of cutting-edge insights, practical tips, and pointers that have relevance for Tae Kwon Do practitioners of all abilities. You will find valuable information that will have immediate relevance to your next sparring session. You will learn variations on certain core techniques that will see you amp your power and speed by upward of 30 percent. You will learn cutting-edge training information that will have you in the best shape of your martial arts career in no time flat. And, above all, you will learn of the many real-world applications of Tae Kwon Do techniques in self-defense situations.

Moreover, you will learn of some of the higher principles that form the foundation of this art and of the characters of the many champions and instructors who have sacrificed so much of their lives living, breathing, sweating, and sharing Tae Kwon Do with all who, like them, see the magnificent potential for positive growth and human understanding that it so richly offers.

—John Little

ULTIMATE GUIDE TO
TAE KWON DO

PART I

History and Traditions

The Force of Chung Do Kwan Tae Kwon Do

Carrying On the Old Ways

By Annellen Simpkins, Ph.D., and Alex Simpkins, Ph.D.

The idealism of the original kwans *(schools) in Korea was unique. It was such an important force that all of Tae Kwon Do practiced throughout the world today derives in some way from these early roots. Of the original nine kwans, Chung Do Kwan, started by Master Won Kook Lee, is generally accepted as first. Its leadership was passed along to Grand Master Duk Sung Son in the 1950s. He took the modest-sized "Blue Wave" school and built it into the largest kwan in Korea. Here is the path that he invites all to follow, even today.*

Following the Japanese occupation (1910–1945), Korea searched for native inspirations to help reawaken its strength of character, which had been submerged under Japanese rule. The government decided to draw upon the power of the indigenous martial arts by uniting all of them together into one national sport. The first conference of the National Board of Advisors for Chung Do Kwan met over dinner on December 9, 1955. Duk Sung Son was an active participant in the process. He attended many top-level meetings with government and military officials and helped to create the sport's new all-encompassing name, Tae Kwon Do, and shape its future.

Over the years, Tae Kwon Do has developed many branches and many styles with different emphases. Nearly every country around the world today practices some form of Tae Kwon Do. People

look at the leaves on the trees and sometimes forget about the roots from which the branches originally grew. Chung Do Kwan has continued the root traditions, carrying on the old ways of training conveyed through the spirit of Grand Master Son. Under his dynamic leadership, Chung Do Kwan Tae Kwon Do has kept its original distinctive nature and developed even further.

Grand Master Son oversees the thriving World Tae Kwon Do Association (WTA), with over 400 schools. Master Jae Bock Chung, in Madison, Wisconsin, serves as the organization's director. Eight other masters oversee regions throughout the United States. A WTA member can go to a school anywhere in the country—from the Stanford University Tae Kwon Do Club on the West Coast to the Harvard University Tae Kwon Do Club on the East Coast— and find the workout faithfully performed in the traditional way, with basics, forms, sparring, and three-step sparring.

Historical Times of Trouble

Now seventy-three, Grand Master Son looks back on the early days and reminisces. "World War II ended and there were many American soldiers around—lieutenants, majors—and they all went to Seoul," he remembers. "It was a lot like Times Square. After the Japanese left Korea, everything was confused. There were many gangsters in Seoul. They threatened people and wielded a great deal of power because the police force was too undeveloped and weak to control all the crime. Fighting was rampant. People used their fists. Soldiers were being knocked out. There was a lot of violence and killing. The kwans stepped in to help the police. Anyone with a black belt in Tae Kwon Do was given an honorary badge. They offered us pistols, but we told them, 'No, we don't need a weapon. We have our Tae Kwon Do.' My students joined in to help keep the peace. Chung Do Kwan had a good reputation, [was] known for power. People respected the honesty, discipline and great strength [of these men]. Koreans were looking for power, hoping to put an end to all the confusion."

Grand Master Son worked with the other schools to build the reputation of Tae Kwon Do in general. "When people saw the patch, they respected it," he says. Through the moral force of Tae Kwon Do, he believes the Koreans were able to find strength and courage to reclaim their country from the havoc of confusion and crime, to rebuild, and to reform.

Son explains how Chung Do Kwan also helped individuals on a personal level. Many youths in this chaotic postwar period found themselves in the middle of the social problems that plagued the country. Much like our troubled youths today, young people in Korea became embroiled in drinking and violence. Grand Master Son helped many to find inner strength and take a positive path in their lives. When he talks, people listen. His influence on his students was and continues to be profound. Their lives change.

"My number one student came into the school one day and told me about a friend who had been taken into a gangster's car the night before and driven away," son recalls. "The young man found himself in a bad area of town with a lot of trouble. Knowing the area and many people, I went down there to look for him. I found him with his hands and neck tied. I questioned him, 'Were you drinking last night?' The young man refused to answer. I reprimanded him firmly. 'What are you doing, going around fighting? This is very bad! Look at you. You aren't so strong. You're weak!' He hung his head, ashamed, and said, 'I'm sorry. Please help.' I replied, 'If I teach you, you cannot go around fighting anymore. You will give Tae Kwon Do a bad name.' After that, he was more humble. He changed his attitude and stayed out of trouble."

Despite all the positive changes that took place in Korea, life was very hard during this period. Grand Master Son was invited by one of his students to come to America to teach. He decided to make the move, and found himself truly welcomed. He explains, "When I first arrived, much of the American teaching was not high caliber. People learned a little karate in the army. When they returned home, they opened a dojang. I arrived in America and the very next day I started teaching!" He found a great demand for his Tae Kwon Do classes. Americans were eager to learn, with four to five people joining every day. He opened satellite schools at Brown University, New York University, West Point, Fordham, and Princeton. He traveled to each site regularly to ensure top-quality teaching. His schools multiplied and his organization grew. Today there are hundreds of schools.

Teaching the Old Ways

Silence Is Golden

Asked if his Tae Kwon Do classes were taught like the classes in Korea, he answers, "I teach the same, the old way. I don't think it will ever change. Always with strong technique. In Chung Do Kwan, basics are done with everybody together, doing their very best, very strong. Then the belts separate into their different levels. Lots of schools do ten minutes of teaching and then talking about their families. You must sweat and concentrate! After a two-hour workout, the whole class is tired! Everybody asks me the same question, 'How do I learn more?' I answer them, 'Practice, practice, practice! No questions, just do your best.'"

Grand Master Son's workouts are grueling when performed as expected. "You must finish a good workout with everybody tired," he says. He is his own best example of these teachings, working up a tremendous sweat in his workouts. That's Chung Do Kwan, Grand Master Son–style. Grand Master Son's philosophy is in the classic tradition of Zen. ("Son" is also the Korean word for Zen.) "Suzuki Roshi [the Japanese philosopher] says it well: 'The more you understand our thinking, the more you find it difficult to talk about it.' The purpose of my talking is to give you some idea of our way, but actually it is not something to talk about, but something to practice. The best way is just to practice without saying anything."

Forms

Grand Master Son's traditional position concerning the meaning of moves in forms is unusual in modern, innovative times. The connection with meaning, in his teaching, is made by doing the form. The practical interpretations or applications of the moves from forms are always secondary. The form transcends its interpretations. He tells his students to be fully attentive, not directing the stream of thought with a particular notion of the moves. To concentrate, emptying the mind while focusing on the motions themselves. Being and doing become one. Then wisdom will come from within. As Suzuki Roshi states, "This kind of thinking is always stable. It is called mindfulness. It is not necessary to make an effort to think in a particular way. Your thinking should not be one-sided. We just think with our whole mind, and see things as they are without any effort."

Interpretations disturb this manner of using the mind, says Son. The experience of the form is primary. Therefore, drilling in the forms themselves comes first, and is always the foundation, the core. Is there any good reason for expounding upon theories in Tae Kwon Do? "When it's late at night and you're too tired to train," responds one of Son's fourth-degree black belts. "I train, then I think over what I learned afterward—for the next six months or so."

Three-Step Sparring

Three-step is a patterned, rhythmical interaction that permits the student to practice block-and-counter combinations with a partner. Whenever you learn a martial art, you learn action and reaction. In three-step, you perfect both sides of this equation. Grand Master Son has unique views on this formal exercise that make it different from other styles that use it. He does not believe that students should learn hundreds of three-steps. Rather, it is best to master a small number of techniques using the basic Tae Kwon Do weapons: blocks, kicks, punches, elbows, and knife-hands. White belts up through the highest-ranked black belts are required to practice the original set of white-belt three-steps. Each block, though moderated carefully while executed, is potentially forceful enough to break an arm when performed at black-belt level. Every counter must be decisive, capable of causing severe damage. Every punch, block, and counter should have speed, focus, accuracy, balance, and power. With years of repetition, practitioners build physical and mental armor to handle the intensity. Tempered with absolute control, pairs of students move back and forth briskly, with no one harmed.

Free-Style Sparring

No-contact sparring sets this style apart from many others. One student recalls, "I've been to dozens of open tournaments. They begin with mini-peewees and on up all day. Anyone can enter as long as they have headgear, hand- and footgear. By 11:00 P.M., kids are lying on the sidelines, noses gushing, parents yelling, 'Kill 'em Johnny!'" Grand Master Son is adamant about no contact in his Tae Kwon Do. The most upset I've seen him is when he sees contact. Usually it happens with brown belts. Their control is not so good. He sees contact, and he is right out there, agitated, saying, "Never this, never, never, never!"

Sparring is the personal expression of all that the student has learned. Grand Master Son feels that specific combinations should not be taught by the instructor. It is for the student to process all that is learned in basics, forms, and three-step and then express it creatively. Freestyle becomes so closely linked to one's core that, as one veteran practitioner said, "You can always tell what kind of day you are having when you get out on the freestyle floor."

The Path

From its very inception to the present day, Chung Do Kwan Tae Kwon Do, through the dynamism of its leader, Grand Master Son, has influenced thousands of students to become better men and women. How does Son's Tae Kwon Do penetrate to the core of the human being? Says one of his many students, "He digs into people; he makes them perform. I come to class from my job sometimes very, very tired. It takes me about an hour and fifteen minutes to travel to Mr. Son's school, and many times I'm tired and really don't feel physically like I want to work out. But when I come here it's like instant pep. Just watching the man pumps the adrenaline through my body and makes me perform." Something he stands for, something he projects, brings out each person's potential. A fourth-degree black belt in his organization once asked her brother, a fellow fifth-degree traveler, "Why do we do this? Why do we go to class every week? Why do we go to these training camps, these seminars? Why do we keep doing this, year after year?" His answer was immediate, direct, and deeply felt: "Why is a rock? Why is a tree?"

Suzuki Roshi wrote, "In our everyday life we are usually trying to change something into something else, or trying to attain something. Just this trying is already in itself an expression of our true nature. Meaning lies in the effort itself." The rest will follow naturally. Therefore, the path is clear.

Alex and Annellen Simpkins are Ph.D.s, black belts, and freelance writers based in San Diego, California. This material originally appeared in the April 1995 issue of Inside Tae Kwon Do *magazine.*

2

The Song Moo Kwan
Its Evolution and Influence

Robert Frankovich

Song Moo Kwan is one of the nine original kwans that merged to form Tae Kwon Do back in 1955. Here, a student and historian of the Song Moo Kwan introduces us to this little-known but highly important Korean martial art. His research suggests an entirely new account of the modern (post–World War II) history of the Korean martial arts.

The ancient history of Korean martial arts has been repeatedly documented in numerous sources, although many questions and controversies still exist. But the modern history of Korean martial arts is another story altogether, being sparsely documented—particularly that era from the end of World War II (1945) to 1955, when the art of Tae Kwon Do was "officially" formed.

Immediately after World War II, a number of Korean martial arts kwans were formed in Korea. Nine of these original kwans merged to form the basis of modern Tae Kwon Do. This is the story of the Song Moo Kwan (or Sang Moo Kwan), one of those nine original schools, and as recently discovered documents suggest, perhaps the very first.

The Origin of Song Moo Kwan

The debate as to which kwan was the first to be established has been the subject of many discussions over the years. Any claims to being "first" are very difficult to verify due to poor communications and record keeping throughout Korea immediately after World War II. Most believe that the Chung Do Kwan dojang, founded by Master Won Kook Lee, was the first to open, in 1945. However, Grand Master Byung Jick Ro, founder of the Song Moo Kwan, opened a dojang in Kaesong, at a *kwan duk gung* (archery school), in mid-1944, actually *during* World War II. Unfortunately, he had to suspend classes after just three months due to a lack of student enrollment.

Nevertheless, this landmark, recorded in Ro's personal papers of the period, has been an overlooked fact in modern Korean martial arts history.

The Kaesong dojang opened upon Grand Master Ro's return from university work in Japan. He had learned Tae Kyon and Su Bak from his neighbors, and had been interested in the defensive techniques that were taught at the local temples. This interest in martial arts lead Ro, during his college years, to search out Gichin Funakoshi, the visionary founder of Shotokan karate who is universally recognized as the father of modern karate. Ro studied under Funakoshi and earned a black belt before returning to Korea. Grand Master Ro's return to Korea was marked by his opening of the Kaesong dojang. Although this first attempt failed, he tried in May 1946 to open a second dojang in Kaesong. This attempt was unsuccessful due to the onset of the Korean War in 1950. Following the Korean War, he finally established a successful dojang in Seoul in 1953. The establishment of the Seoul dojang, rather than Kaesong dojang, is mistakenly accepted as marking the emergence of Song Moo Kwan as one of the nine original kwans.

It should be noted that other than the first attempt in Kaesong, which was in an archery school, Song Moo Kwan was taught in its own dojang. The only other kwan to do this was the Chung Do Kwan. The rest of the post–World War II kwans that came into being were taught within YMCA-type organizations where they would rent space in which to teach classes.

The Origin of Tae Kwon Do: New Historic Facts

For decades, historians have believed that the formation of Tae Kwon Do on April 11, 1955, was the first universal merger of post–World War II Korean martial arts. That is inaccurate, according to Ro's documents. Two years earlier, on May 25, 1953, the grand masters of the nine kwans attended a conference which concluded with the establishment of the Korean Kung Soo Do Association. This was the first organization developed by the Korean martial arts community. This association did not elect a president, but installed the following masters in the following positions in addition to recognizing one representative from each kwan:

Vice President
Young Joo Cho (possibly Yudo, Korean for judo)

Executive Director
Byung Jick Ro (Song Moo Kwan)

Directors
Hwang Kee (Moo Duk Kwan)
Chung Woo Lee (Ji Do Kwan)
Yon Kue Pyang (Chi Do Kwan)
Jong Myung Hyon (Chung Do Kwan)

The association placed Grand Master Ro in the chairmanship of the Rank Promotion Committee and as the Master Instructor. The most important decision made by this association may have been the adoption of the name *Tae Kwon Do*, which was presented to them by General Hong Hi Choi as the formal name for the arts taught by these nine kwans.

The First Influential Organizations

In November 1958, Hwang Kee Hwang, founder of the Tang Soo Do Moo Duk Kwan, withdrew from the Kung Soo Do Association and established the Korean Tang Soo Do Association. Grand Master Hwang petitioned the Korean Amateur Sports Association (KASA) to become a member of that organization, but was refused due to the lack of unity being presented by the original kwans.

The Korean Kung Soo Do Association and the Korean Tang Soo Do Association met in July 1959 and created the Soo Bahk Do Association. This new organization attempted to petition the KASA for membership, with the claim that it contained all of the original kwans in one united group. But they, too, were refused.

This is the same time period in which General Choi became president of Oh Do Kwan, which had emerged in 1953 with Jong Myung Hyon as its leader. General Choi and the Soo Bahk Do Association held a conference in September 1959. This lead to the formation of the influential Korean Tae Kwon Do Association (KTA). Shortly after the KTA was established, grand masters Hwang and Yon Kue Pyang left the organization, apparently for political reasons, and have remained separate ever since.

Another problem that had arisen was the loss of several grand masters, for different reasons, including being missing in action after the Korean War. This left the students to fill the vacancies and carry on the traditions. This loss is why Hee Sang Ro, Grand Master Ro's son, claims that his father could be considered the "supreme" grand master of Tae Kwon Do. This status should be further considered, according to Hee Sang Ro, because his father is the only grand master who is still actively involved with Tae Kwon Do.

The KASA accepted the petition for membership of the KTA in June 1962, through the help of General Choi. Grand Master Ro became president of the KTA from 1966 to 1967, and also served as the chairman of the Rank Promotion Committee from 1962 to 1969. Throughout that time—and to this day—Grand Master Ro has dedicated his life to the promotion and expansion of Tae Kwon Do.

During the early 1970s, with the formation of the new and powerful World Tae Kwon Do Federation, the Korean hierarchy sought to establish a single martial art as Korea's national art and sport. Consequently, the various kwans were given numbers and their formal names were eliminated. This loss of identity may have been executed, in part, to demonstrate unity of the kwans once South Korean president Park Chung Hee proclaimed that Tae Kwon Do was to be the national sport. Now there was simply one art, called universally "Tae Kwon Do." Today, as more students are searching for the roots and traditions of their schools and instructors, more and more may decide to resume using the original kwan name in the identification of their particular school.

Song Moo Kwan in the United States

Song Moo Kwan expanded to the United States in the 1960s. Grand Master Ro did not set up specific regions or assign instructors to certain locations, which consequently allowed the Song Moo Kwan pioneers the freedom to establish a dojang wherever an instructor chose. Some of the notable Song Moo Kwan instructors are: Master Il Joo Kim (Cleveland, Ohio); Master Moo Myung Yun (Willmar, Minnesota); Master Byung Yul Lee (Maple Grove, Minnesota); Master Joon Pyo Choi (Columbus, Ohio); Master Yong Kyu Yu (Houston, Texas); Master Chang Jin Kang (California); Master Jin Il Chang (New York); and Master Tae Ryang Chang (New Jersey).

Another instructor who deserves mention is the now-retired Master Jay Hyon. Master Hyon moved into the Minneapolis, Minnesota, area and opened the Karate Center dojang. He played a large part in bringing Tae Kwon Do into Minnesota. He also played a role in bringing Grand Master Ro to the United States. Master Hyon retired in 1980 and turned his teaching responsibilities over to Master Hee Sang Ro, the Grand Master's son, who had come over from Korea four years earlier. Master Ro continues to develop Tae Kwon Do and carry on the traditions of Song Moo Kwan through his North American Tae Kwon Do Federation (NATF). He has also been working on the development of a more organized Song Moo Kwan community, which would include a central promotion committee.

Currently you can find Song Moo Kwan instructors as members of a multitude of Tae Kwon Do associations and federations. This comes partly from Grand Master Ro's belief in personal development taking a greater role than the politics of rank. In fact, you will find that a variety of *poomsae* (forms) are taught within the Song Moo Kwan community, including Pinan, Chang Quan, Taeguek, and Chung Bong. The Chung Bong poomsae are unique to Song Moo Kwan; they were developed by Master Hyon and first performed in 1974. These poomsae were designed to be realistic yet allow for some of the flashy kicking techniques that can be found in Tae Kwon Do. The seven poomsae in this set were developed so the majority of the combinations within them could be quickly and easily adapted to fit within combat situations. They also include the symmetry that ensures each student will develop in a balanced manner.

Lastly, jumping and spinning kicks can be found, as well as stances that fit combat and tournament situations, and a variety of hand techniques. There are no official poomsae for Song Moo Kwan. Although poomsae play an important role in the development of a Tae Kwon Do student, the decision of which set to study is less consequential. All poomsae are intended to build the student's stamina, endurance, and technique, so which patterns are learned does not have a significant effect on the student's abilities.

The Song Moo Kwan has developed at an outstanding rate. The NATF has about twenty-five schools listed and the Northern Tae Kwon Do Association, headed by Tom Sullivan (one of Master Hyon's students), has schools numbering in the sixties. The success of these groups is most likely similar to other groups throughout the country. The years of Tae Kwon Do growth in the United States have helped the art as a whole grow successfully. Unfortunately, along with this growth there have been many political battles that have hurt the students.

The continued growth of Tae Kwon Do requires that its masters and instructors go back and review the five tenets of Tae Kwon Do: integrity, courtesy, perseverance, self-control, and indomitable spirit. Many instructors teach these concepts, but do not always "walk their talk" when dealing with other instructors or organizations. Instructors who maintain these tenets can teach their students the more important aspects of life, instead of demonstrating greed and self-importance. When the international organizations return to practicing the tenets outside the dojang as well as inside, then we may be able to develop the kind of community and society that we are preaching. This would also lead to smaller victories—such as keeping Tae Kwon Do a part of the Olympics.

Robert Frankovich of Superior, Wisconsin, is a third-degree black belt in Song Moo Kwan and a first-degree black belt registered with the World Tae Kwon Do Federation. This material originally appeared in the December 1994 issue of Inside Tae Kwon Do *magazine. The author respectfully thanks Master Hee Sang Ro for his assistance and the translation of his father's notes.*

3

The History of Tang Soo Do

John Hancock

Like so many other martial arts, Tang Soo Do's history is a mystery. Because there are few well–documented facts, this popular Korean martial art is subject to oral tradition and speculation. Here, a Tang Soo Do black belt and Kentucky police officer uses his expert investigative skills to unravel some of the mysteries behind his art.

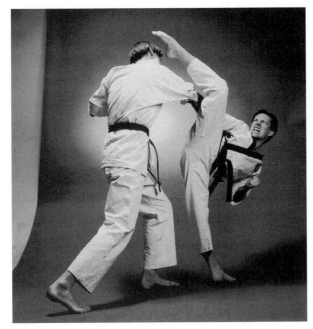

Tang Soo Do black belt Dave Macomber (right) possesses the dexterity to kick high—even during infighting!

Unlocking the history and development of ancient martial arts is no small challenge. One cannot rely solely upon the oral tradition of the school. While the oral tradition does provide clues found nowhere else, it is often sketchy and inconsistent with documented fact. Observation of the style may provide information, yet style is very subjective and relies upon the interpretation of the practitioner, much the same as the oral tradition.

Nearly all forms of ancient martial arts maintain a living catalog of their practice through *hyung* or forms. These, too, can provide clues about an art's history and development. But once again, it is the interpretation of the practitioner that affects the practice and history of the forms. Unlocking the mystery of a martial art's history requires the ability to step outside the womb of the school; to cross examine the oral tradition; to search out fact through examination of other histories, sciences, and cultures; and to correlate these with the oral tradition in order to deduce the truth. Sometimes, one must settle for a hypothesis based upon these correlations.

According to oral tradition, Tang Soo Do is over two thousand years old. It is based upon techniques the Korean people adopted from Chinese warriors of the Tang dynasty, blended with the native arts of Soo Bahk and Tae Kyon. It was also influenced by military fighting skills known as Kwon Bup. The art was resurrected in 1945 by Hwang Kee, who founded the Moo Duk Kwan school. Grand Master Hwang, through self-study, combined Korean arts he learned from books with arts he learned in China. The many hyung used by the school are either Grand Master Hwang's creations or were brought by him from China. With this oral tradition, we begin the search.

Question after question emerges as one delves deeper and deeper, and, like an onion, as one layer is peeled away, another is found: Where does the term "Tang Soo Do" originate? Where did Soo Bahk and Tae Kyon come from? What is Kwon Bup? How did these arts become part of Tang Soo Do? Where did Grand Master Hwang learn these arts? What is the history of Tang Soo Do's hyung? Why does Tang Soo Do bear such a resemblance to karate? Why are the forms of Tang Soo Do and karate virtually the same? Through examination of the history of Korea and its Asian neighbors, we discover that there are three distinct chapters in Tang Soo Do's evolution: ancient history; the influential Japanese occupation of Korea from 1910 to 1945; and the "modern myths" that appear after 1945.

Ancient History

To understand where Tang Soo Do comes from, you must look back to the history of the Asian continent and the peninsula we know today as Korea. We begin during the period known as the Three Kingdoms (57 B.C.–A.D. 935). This period is named for three great states that developed on the Korean Peninsula during this time: Koguryo (37 B.C.–A.D. 668); Paekche (18 B.C.–A.D. 660); and Silla (57 B.C.–A.D. 935). For over 500 years, each of these nations grew and developed. Each had periods of war and of peace with one another. Each had its own internal problems and triumphs. Each had contact with greater and lesser neighbors in Asia. It is not until 618 A.D. that this history becomes vitally important to Tang Soo Do.

China was ruled by the Sui dynasty from A.D. 589–618. During the early seventh century, the Tang rose to power and overthrew the Sui to found the Tang dynasty (A.D. 618–906). During the Tang dynasty, many advancements were made in the Chinese martial arts. It was during this period that the early forms of t'ai chi were being created and the Shaolin monks were making their kung fu famous.

In Korea, political power moves and alliances were being made as Silla began to grow in power. Silla's Hwarang warriors (elite knights; literally, "flowering youth") were in their glory, and Silla's neighbors recognized the threat of such a fighting force on their borders. Paekche and Koguryo struck an alliance. Paekche also formed agreements with Japan. Silla, suddenly surrounded by hostile countries on all sides, struck an accord with Tang China.

The Tang and Koguryo had been antagonistic toward each other for many years. In 645 A.D. the Tang fought an unsuccessful war against Koguryo. But Silla, backed by their strong friends in China, attacked and conquered Paekche in 660 A.D. The resources of Paekche were absorbed, and in 668 A.D. Silla and the Tang army attacked and overran Koguryo. Silla unified the peninsula for the first time. Only the Par Hae to the far north remained outside their control.

Silla's victory was short lived. Once the Koguryo fell, the Tang army could not be convinced to leave the peninsula. Silla brilliantly elicited the assistance of the nations they themselves had vanquished and, together as one people, they forced the Tang army out of the country. After the wars ended, Silla grew and developed a unified culture in Korea. Many aspects of Chinese culture and government were adopted. Silla skillfully negotiated peace with Tang China and active trade began between them. Many Koreans went to China to receive higher education. From their earlier alliance, the Hwarang had already absorbed many tactics and techniques from the Tang army. Tae Kyon, as a fighting form, was already present in Koguryo, and the Hwarang combined this art with skills learned from the Tang. The Hwarang occasionally referred to their art as Tang Soo Ki ("tang hand techniques").

In the latter part of the ninth century, the Hwarang grew fat, lazy, and incompetent, without compassion for the people. Civil unrest grew until General Wang Kon led an insurrection in 918 A.D., founding the Koryo nation. In 926 A.D. Koryo conquered Par Hae. With popular backing, Wang Kon convinced the last Silla king to surrender peacefully in 935 A.D., and the Koryo dynasty was founded. It is from this dynasty that we derive the modern name Korea.

The area north of Koryo was known as Khi Tan (today we know it as Manchuria). From A.D. 994–1018, the Khi Tan attempted to invade Koryo. General Kang Kam Chan led the Koryo army against the Khi Tan in 1018 A.D. and destroyed their forces. Following the war, Koryo built its own "great wall" across the northern border of the peninsula. The Koryo dynasty would stand until 1392.

The Chinese Influence

During the reign of Koryo, dynasties came and went in China. In 906 the Tang fell and the Sung dynasty was formed. During the Sung dynasty, a famous martial artist known as Chang San Feng (Chang Sam Bong in Korea) developed and formalized t'ai chi ch'uan ("grand supreme fist"). Also during the Sung dynasty, General Yeuh Fei created the styles of eagle-claw kung fu and Hsing I Ch'uan ("mind form fist").

Yeuh Fei instituted the instruction of Hsing I Ch'uan to all soldiers in the Sung army.

The Koryo and Sung enjoyed a generous friendship with one another. During this time the Koreans began to refer to their indigenous fighting arts as Soo Bahk Ki ("hand striking techniques"), while Chinese arts were sometimes referred to as Kwon Bup ("fist method"). Korea and China exchanged their military knowledge along with cultural, political, and social inventions.

North of China, Genghis Khan and the Mongols began amassing strength and in 1225 A.D. overran China to found the Yuan dynasty. The Mongols attempted to force Koryo to turn against their Chinese friends. When Koryo refused, the army of Khan began pouring into northern Koryo. General Kan Kam Chan led the Koryo warriors against the Mongol horde and defeated them. Koryo was the only nation to stand against Genghis Khan's army and win.

In 1368, the last of the khans lost power and the Ming dynasty (A.D. 1368–1644) was formed. In Korea, poor advisement from Buddhist monks with their own political agenda convinced the Koryo king to order his army to attack Ming China in support of the Mongols. General Yi Song Kye, realizing the folly of such a move, instead turned his troops on the capital and overthrew the Koryo government. The last dynasty of Korea, the Chosun, or Yi, dynasty, was founded in 1392.

During the Chosun dynasty (A.D. 1392–1910), Korea saw many of its greatest achievements in science and culture. Leaders such as King Se Jong and Admiral Yi Sun Sin inspired the nation with their vision, knowledge, wisdom, and valor. In 1790 A.D., Lee Duk Moo completed a text of martial art techniques learned during the Koryo dynasty, so that this valuable knowledge would be preserved. This text, known as the *Moo Yae Dobo Tong Ji*, became the guide for educating and training the soldiers of Chosun. Written in four volumes, one of which is devoted solely to Kwon Bup, this classic documents the influence of Chinese martial arts on the warrior skills of Korea.

The Chosun dynasty enjoyed peaceful relations with its neighbors for many years. In the latter part of the eighteenth century, Korea began to have its first contacts with the Western world. Finding much of our religion and culture abrasive to their established society, Chosun closed its doors to foreign relations and earned the nickname the "Hermit Kingdom." Gradually, Western and Japanese pressures pried open Korea. The Japanese began a calculated plan of expansion into Korea and Manchuria at the close of the eighteenth century. Finally, in 1910, Japan annexed Korea in its entirety and occupied the country.

The Japanese Occupation

Japan held Korea in a virtual vise grip from 1910 to 1945. It is important for the modern student of martial arts to understand the scope and extent of this oppression. During this period an entire generation of Koreans was born and grew up in a Japanese-dominated society. Korean culture was gradually put to death. Koreans were forbidden their own dress, language, customs, and education. Treasures of the nation were seized, and historical artifacts, records, and books were destroyed, leaving much of Korean history obscure today. Korean families who would have any quality of life had to adapt and conform to a Japanese standard. Young Koreans were raised according to a Japanese agenda, and obtained their higher education in Japanese schools. The Japanese also banned the practice of indigenous martial arts. The only martial arts openly practiced were those the Japanese brought to Korea, or that Koreans brought back from study in Japan. All of this was in an effort to absorb Korea into the Japanese empire.

In no other time period was Korea so totally influenced by another nation. But it is these very Japanese influences, especially when it comes to mar-

tial arts, that many Korean martial arts masters most adamantly disown. Hwang Kee seems no different.

The Modern Myths

At the conclusion of World War II, Korea was liberated by the United States when Japan surrendered in 1945. In the first year of liberation, many Koreans returned home from Japan, China, and elsewhere. Very soon, Korean martial artists began teaching in their own schools. Much of what we know about the origins of these schools, and the arts they teach, comes to us as oral traditions passed on by the founders. Of interest to Tang Soo Do practitioners is the history of Hwang Kee and his Moo Duk Kwan school.

Hwang Kee was born in 1913 along the 38th parallel of Korea, an area today known as the DMZ (Demilitarized Zone), which separates North and South Korea. As a young man, Hwang attended military school. Through family friends, he was able to see and practice indigenous Korean martial arts such as Tae Kyon. Purportedly, an uncle trained Hwang in Soo Bahk Ki. Hwang also studied the ancient military text *Moo Yea Dobo Tong Ji* and trained himself in Kwon Bup. Hwang was reputed to have been an accomplished martial artist at age twenty-two. It is also related through the oral tradition that Hwang was arrested by the Japanese for his involvement in these banned martial arts practices.

In 1936 A.D., Hwang left Korea and traveled into Manchuria. Touring China, Hwang studied many martial arts and attended a Chinese kung fu school where he studied *kuo shu* (Chinese boxing). After Korea's liberation in 1945, Hwang returned home and took up work for the railroad. On November 9, 1945, Hwang opened his first martial arts school in the Seoul railway station and called it the Moo Duk Kwan ("martial virtue school"). Hwang referred to his art as Tang Soo Do ("Chinese hand way"). In 1953, Hwang formed the Korean Tang Soo Do Association. After an unsuccessful attempt to merge with other kwans in 1960, Hwang formed the Korean Soo Bahk Do Association and began to refer to his art as Soo Bahk Do.

Hwang has claimed his Moo Duk Kwan teaches an art based upon Tae Kyon, Soo Bahk Ki, Kwon Bup, and Chinese martial arts. Hwang and his followers refute claims that their Tang Soo Do is based upon Japanese karate. The school claims the forms they use (which resemble karate kata) were all learned by Grand Master Hwang in China.

Cross-Examination

Modern practitioners of martial arts have noted the striking similarities between Tang Soo Do and karate, the Shotokan karate-do school has claimed for years that Tang Soo Do is merely a copy of their system. The Moo Duk Kwan vehemently denies this. While it would be an overgeneralization to say Tang Soo Do is merely Korean karate, some facts do bear examination.

Hwang himself states he attended military school as a youth. We must remember that Hwang was born and grew up during the Japanese occupation of Korea. Any school he attended—especially a military school—would have been under Japanese supervision. The founder of the Chung Do Kwan, Won Kook Lee, reportedly operated a martial arts school, unofficially, as far back as 1933. Lee referred to his art as Tang Soo Do and claimed it was based on Shotokan karate-do, which he learned in Japan while attending school. It is likely Hwang and Won Kook Lee exchanged knowledge in these early days. Both men opened schools in Seoul in 1945 and had associations with one another in those early days of the formation of the kwans.

Hwang states he was pressured by the Japanese because of his practice of native Korean martial arts. Hwang was allegedly arrested for this crime. This is quite plausible. However, it is unlikely Hwang was imprisoned, issued a death sentence, or escaped from a Japanese jail as is often claimed. Hwang states that he left Korea in 1936 and traveled to Manchuria to escape the pressures of Japanese influence, and that while there, he studied Chinese martial arts. Yet, Japan occupied Manchuria at the turn of the century as oppressively as it did Korea. He also says he worked for the railroad—not mentioned is that it was the Japanese who built the railways into Manchuria as part of their imperial supply lines. It would appear then that Hwang worked for the Japanese. However, it is likely Hwang was ordered into this work by the Japanese—perhaps as a punishment for practicing Korean martial arts.

Many famous karate masters were also in Manchuria at the same time as Hwang. It has been rumored that Hwang claimed Gogen Yamaguchi (Japanese Goju-ryu karate-do founder) as a personal friend. Yamaguchi was a Japanese intelligence officer stationed in Manchuria near the Russian border in 1939. We know Hwang was also near the Russian border at one point in his travels, by an anecdote in which the town of Man Chu Li is mentioned. In his book, *Tang Soo Do / Soo Bahk Do* (1978), Hwang credits much of his knowledge of Japanese karate history to a Mr. Kon Do. (Perhaps this is Professor Kinjo of Japan, a noted historian of martial arts.) Hwang also mentions a Mr. Humakoshy (Gichin Funakoshi, founder of Shotokan karate-do) and Mr. Maboo Mi (Kenwa Mabuni, founder of Shito-ryu karate-do). This is interesting because Won Kook Lee (of Chung Do Kwan Tang Soo Do) based his art on Shotokan, and Goju-ryu karate's Gogen Yamaguchi, Hwang's purported friend, has ties to Shito-ryu founder Kenwa Mabuni. Additionally, Hwang mentions Masters I Dos (Yasutsune Itosu, a.k.a. Anko Itosu) and Hiasionna (Kanryo Higaonna). Both these masters taught Kenwa Mabuni.

Other facts raise questions among the hyungs practiced by the Moo Duk Kwan. Hwang's son, Hyun Chul Hwang, has stated his father learned the forms while studying in Manchuria. Keep in mind, a plethora of Japanese masters was in Manchuria at the same time. Hwang states the Pyeongan series of forms were created by Master I Dos, who simplified the Jae Nam form while studying and teaching in China. However, I Dos was an Okinawan educator who studied karate. Records state I Dos did simplify a Chinese form known as Chiang Nan into the five Pinan katas and began teaching them to elementary school students in Okinawa in 1901 as a form of physical education. Research does not indicate that I Dos studied in China, but rather that he studied from Chinese living on Okinawa.

Another rumor that has come directly out of the Moo Duk Kwan is that in the 1950's, Hwang traveled to Japan and Okinawa to study their martial arts. Claims have been made by karate practitioners that records exist on Okinawa documenting Hwang's visit and study.

The advanced forms of Tang Soo Do, as taught by the Moo Duk Kwan, do point to a Chinese influence. The form Tae Kuk Kwan means "t'ai chi ch'uan," and the form Jang Kwon means "long fist." Both are virtually indistinguishable from their Chinese counterparts. In Hwang's book, diagrams and text explain exercises from a much older Chinese book, *Yuk Keun Kyung* (*I Chin Ching*, literally, "*Muscle Change Classic*"). These exercises are attributed to the Shaolin temple school and are forms of Chi Kung. Many of the basic movements of Tang Soo Do, as practiced today, are similar to Hsing I Ch'uan kung fu. Tang Soo Do masters visiting China in recent years have commented that the form Bal Che is strikingly similar to mainland practices.

Conclusions

Is Tang Soo Do a copy of Japanese karate? Not hardly. Does it incorporate elements from Japanese and Okinawan karate? Most assuredly. Is there a Chinese influence in Tang Soo Do? Most definitely. Is Tang Soo Do based upon Tae Kyon, Soo Bahk Ki, and Kwon Bup? Without a doubt, yes. As for questions concerning Hwang's personal training and instruction, only Hwang himself can say for sure. Nonetheless, Tang Soo Do will continue to evolve and grow under the new influence of American masters who have taken this art into their hearts and souls. So long as Tang Soo Do is passed on with its philosophy of justice and tenets of integrity, it will continue to prosper.

John Hancock is a fourth dan in Tang Soo Do who also holds a black belt in Shorin-ryu karate-do, has studied the Korean sword art of Sim Do Kwan, and has trained and lived in Seoul, Korea. He works as a full-time police officer and lives in LaGrange, Kentucky. This material originally appeared in the April 1994 issue of Inside Tae Kwon Do *magazine.*

The Difference Between Tang Soo Do and Tae Kwon Do

Jane Hallander

Many Americans mistakenly believe that Tang Soo Do and Tae Kwon Do are different names for the same martial art. In reality, though both arts originated in Korea, they are two distinct systems with more differences than similarities.

For generations, people have asked, "Which came first, the chicken or the egg?" Many Americans think Korean martial arts have the same dilemma—Tang Soo Do or Tae Kwon Do? A common misconception is that these two styles are one and the same.

Hyeon Kon Lee of Herndon, Virginia, has the answers. Lee is a seventh-degree black belt with the World Tae Kwon Do Association, but he started his martial arts career in Tang Soo Do. He is also the head of the Eagle Tae Kwon Do Federation, with several schools on the East Coast. Lee says most Tae Kwon Do masters who are today in their late 30s and older started as Tang Soo Do practitioners and in later years changed to Tae Kwon Do. The reason for this lies in recent history.

Theories of Development: Myth or Fact?

In 1933, Won Kook Lee founded Tang Soo Do, but not as an official organization. (Won Kook Lee is usually credited with founding Chung Do Kwan in the 1940s.) Won Kook Lee studied karate in Japan during Japan's occupation of Korea, and based his new Korean art on the popular Japanese martial art Shotokan karate. Soon, many Tang Soo Do associations sprang up throughout Korea with masters who had studied in China, Japan, and Korea.

After the Korean Conflict (1950–1953), General Hong Hi Choi designed a new martial art for the military, based on the ancient Korean martial art Tae Kyon. He called his new style "tae kwon do" ("foot and fist way"). As Tae Kwon Do became more popular, Tang Soo Do associations started calling themselves Tae Kwon Do associations. Only the Moo Duk Kwan organization of Hwang Kee stayed with the name Tang Soo Do. Hwang formed an official Tang Soo Do association and became known as the founder of Tang Soo Do. Although the style was called Tang Soo Do before Hwang adopted the name, it was Hwang who secured the official sanction and backing of the Korean government for Tang Soo Do.

That's the modern history. One version of ancient history has Tang Soo Do coming to Korea from Tang dynasty China during Korea's Three Kingdoms period (the third and fourth centuries A.D.); according to the storytellers, Tang Soo Do means "Tang dynasty hands." However, Hyeon Kon Lee does not subscribe to that version. According to him, during the Three Kingdoms era the Koguryo kingdom's first king conquered Manchuria. That required an army of trained fighters. According to Lee, formal military training—originating at home, not China—was probably the root of all ancient Korean martial arts.

Lee also rejects the notion that either Tae Kwon Do or Tang Soo Do has Buddhist roots. He does believe that, for survival, many desperate martial artists hid and trained in Buddhist temples, which were so-called "safe zones." Since Buddhism has greatly influenced Korea and its culture, people find it easy to attribute all martial arts' origins to Buddhism. But were either the Buddhism or the Tang-dynasty-hands explanation true, it would be an overwhelming coincidence that Tang Soo Do forms are almost identical to Japanese Shotokan karate katas. Lee attributes this to the fact that many early Tang Soo Do masters studied martial arts in Japan.

Tang Soo Do forms have not changed through the years. Tae Kwon Do forms that once resembled karate have been altered to conform with the ancient Korean martial arts.

Tae Kwon Do and Tang Soo Do: A Study in Contrasts

Sport, or Martial Art?

The basic difference between Tang Soo Do and Tae Kwon Do is that Tang Soo Do adheres to the traditional way, emphasizing practical martial art, while Tae Kwon Do emphasizes sport. Hwang Kee tried to make Tang Soo Do relate directly to practical martial arts and self-defense. True Tang Soo Do practitioners do not consider themselves in the same category as Tae Kwon Do practitioners. They say Tang Soo Do is Korea's *martial art* and Tae Kwon Do is Korea's *sport*. There's something to this premise. Tae Kwon Do has been in the public eye, openly funded by the Korean government, until it has evolved into a Korean national sport. Many people are involved in the sporting and tournament aspects of Tae Kwon Do to the point where they train only to win championships. Of course, many Tae Kwon Do instructors teach Tae Kwon Do as a traditional martial art and as a sport.

Techniques

While the original practice of Tae Kwon Do used pressure points, throwing, grappling techniques, and weapons, Tang Soo Do stylists maintain that because of Tae Kwon Do's heavy emphasis on sport, its practitioners no longer understand these aspects. That's what gives Tae Kwon Do the reputation of being a kicking and punching martial art that excludes the more subtle techniques. The other side of this argument is that by sticking to the traditional way and refusing change, Tang Soo Do stylists have slowed improvement of their martial arts skills, since change often results in improvements, while no change results in stagnation.

In keeping with the tradition of practical, no-nonsense martial arts, Tang Soo Do employs joint-locks and pressure-point techniques. Because these techniques aren't emphasized, as in Hapkido or Kuk Sool, jointlocks and pressure point stimulation are often passed off as an addition to Tang Soo Do, called *ho shin mu sool*. Actually, these techniques belong as much to Tang Soo Do as they do to any other self-defense style. Tang Soo Do stylists also train with some weapons, but unlike in most traditional martial arts training, most weapons training in Tang Soo Do addresses how to defend *against* weapons, not how to *use* weapons. There are several weapons forms in Tang Soo Do. However, weapons defense techniques are emphasized over forms practice.

Stances

Because Tang Soo Do is patterned after Japanese karate, its stances are wider than Tae Kwon Do stances. Most of the weight is placed on the back leg, with the upper body tilted slightly backward in a position resembling karate's back stance. Only the side of the body faces the target, exposing few vulnerable areas. Tae Kwon Do stances no longer resemble those used in Tang Soo Do. The trend has been toward shorter, more upright stances for better mobility and speed, especially in tournament sparring. The Tae Kwon Do stylist's weight is more evenly placed between front and back feet, with the body facing the target at a less severe angle. The fighter's upper body rests directly between front and back legs, allowing more speed and mobility in all directions.

Kicks

Kicking style remains a big difference between Tang Soo Do and Tae Kwon Do. The basic kicks are similar. However, Tae Kwon Do has a much greater variety. In Tae Kwon Do's early days, only a few kicks were emphasized and mastered. Through the years, Tae Kwon Do stylists have added more aerial kicks, running kicks, 180- and 360-degree turning kicks,

and combination kicks until today there are over 100 different kicking and punching combinations.

Tang Soo Do still emphasizes only a few traditional kicks. Originally, Tang Soo Do had a front kick, side kick, and something half-way between a front kick and a roundhouse. These were the same three basic kicks seen in Japanese karate systems.

Among those three basic kicks, Tang Soo Do's front kick is similar to Tae Kwon Do's front kick; only the hand and body positions are different. Tang Soo Do stylists drop their hands back as they thrust their hips forward into the kick. Tae Kwon Do practitioners bring their hands up to protect their head and chest while tilting their bodies slightly forward into the kick. Tang Soo Do's side kick is a stepping side kick designed to build momentum and power as the Tang Soo Do stylist steps toward the target. Tae Kwon Do's standing side kick simply requires the practitioner to lift the knee and launch the kick, saving time and extra movement. While Tang Soo Do uses body mass and momentum to carry kicking power, Tae Kwon Do stylists lift their knees high and thrust their hips into the kick for power. Today's Tang Soo Do also employs a roundhouse kick similar to Tae Kwon Do's. The basic difference is that Tang Soo Do stylists step into the kick with the same cross-step pattern used for the side kick. Tae Kwon Do stylists just raise their knee high and kick.

Punches

Tang Soo Do's hand techniques still resemble those used in karate, employing straight, forward-moving power techniques. The primary fist technique is a reverse punch, similar to karate's reverse punch. Tae Kwon Do hand techniques have more variety. According to Lee, today's Tae Kwon Do hand techniques are similar to Western boxing, using the basic principles of traditional techniques, but with much more snap and speed. Tae Kwon Do hand actions also include not only straight punches, but punches aimed at the side rather than the centerline and often directed in short speedy circles.

the best features of the martial arts is that there is something for everyone.

Conclusion

Tang Soo Do and Tae Kwon Do are as different as night and day in purpose and technique. Tae Kwon Do reflects the changing face of modernization, while Tang Soo Do represents practical traditionalism. There's nothing wrong with either view. One of

Jane Hallander is a veteran martial arts writer and a regular contributor to CFW Enterprises publications. This material originally appeared in the July 1988 edition of Inside Karate *magazine.*

5

An Interview with Grand Master General Hong Hi Choi

Susan Richards

General Hong Hi Choi is president of the International Tae Kwon Do Federation (ITF).
Now in his 80s, General Choi is recognized by many aficionados as the founder of the art
of Tae Kwon Do; he has dedicated his life to teaching it.

With a travel schedule that would exhaust a man half his age, General Hong Hi Choi travels the globe giving seminars and promoting his art. Born in Korea in 1918, the general has lived a fascinating life with an outstanding military career that could be a book in itself. *The Encyclopedia of Tae Kwon Do*, a fifteen-volume work written by General Choi, is considered a technical masterpiece. Assisting in this rare interview is Master Rhee Ki Ha, eighth *dan* (black-belt rank) and vice president of the ITF. Master Rhee is a pioneer of Tae Kwon Do in Great Britain and Singapore. Also assisting are Master Choi Jung Hwa, General Choi's son and the ITF undersecretary of general planning; and Master Tom MacCallum, ITF undersecretary general.

You are recognized as the Father of Tae Kwon Do. How many countries are in the Tae Kwon Do family now?

Well, I'm a big father! Over forty million of my sons and daughters worldwide [are] under the banner of the ITF. It's a big family! We are a family organization, for the first time in human history. You cannot find a stronger organization.

Today, many women and children are training in Tae Kwon Do. How do you feel about this?

That is very nice. I always say, if a woman wants to train in Tae Kwon Do, I say try it. Children eventually become old. When they are young, they

Left to right: Master Rhee Ki Ha, General Choi, Master Tom MacCallum, and Master Choi Jung Hwa in Malaysia in 1994.

learn very fast. They can become champions of freedom and justice. Not only that, but they will become wonderful, outstanding instructors, you see. So, we emphasize children, beginning at age seven or eight.

What makes Tae Kwon Do stand out from other martial arts?

For the founder, this is very hard to answer. Master Rhee, the Vice President, will answer.

Master Rhee Ki Ha: Do you know of any other martial art whose founder is still in this present world? Tae Kwon Do is the only one. The other martial arts, all they have is history, [and] some people interpret this differently, so they have different styles. But in Tae Kwon Do, we don't claim any style, we just still follow and improve it. This is our big privilege. Only we can take advantage of our founder still [being] in this world, so we are still learning and improving, progressing and promoting.

Master Choi Jung Hwa: Tae Kwon Do is known for its technical excellence over the other martial arts. Technical excellence meaning constant development and advancement in the arena of the martial arts. Unfortunately, the other arts, although advanced in their period, do not have their founders still on this earth, so their technical development stopped from that time on. Whereas Tae Kwon Do is constantly being improved by the founder himself, which is handed down to us. That is why it stands out. We consider ourselves the luckiest martial artists in the world to still be training with the founder himself.

General Hong Hi Choi: I have not much money, you see, but I have plenty of first-class instructors. In 1955, there was only one Hong Hi Choi. Today, there are hundreds of thousands of General Chois, all over the world. They are first-class instructors. Our standard is that a student can only excel under a qualified instructor. You cannot find big bamboo in the little field; big bamboo only grows in the big bamboo field. So Tae Kwon Do spreads like wild-fire all over the world. In thirty-nine years, Tae Kwon Do has covered the entire world. [That's because] Tae Kwon Do people say every movement is designed scientifically so that anyone can learn and teach scientifically very fast. That is the advantage of Tae Kwon Do.

What makes you happiest about Tae Kwon Do?

My dream has become a reality; that is, the utmost fantasy of spreading and teaching Tae Kwon Do regardless of race, religion, nationality, or ideological boundaries. I do not hesitate to say I am the happiest man alive.

Susan Richards, first dan, owns and operates ARA *Tae Kwon Do in Dover, Delaware. This material originally appeared in the March 1995 edition of* Inside Tae Kwon Do *magazine.*

PART II

Training

6

Tae Kwon Do's One-Step Sparring

Jane Hallander

In college we learn formulas to use to solve mathematical problems. Tae Kwon Do's one-step sparring is a formula used to solve a self-defense problem. Although a defense situation is not exactly the same as the original one-step pattern, one-step sparring is the foundation that develops defense reactions.

All martial arts have their own ways to teach students freestyle sparring and self-defense. Some teach the basics of self-defense through forms practice. Others prefer that their followers put on hand and foot protection and experience sparring firsthand. While each method has its merits, Tae Kwon Do practitioners have their own style of guiding students into mastering self-defense and sparring situations. It's called "one-step sparring" and bears some resemblance to individual technique training, except that one-step sparring is closer to freestyle training.

Miami Beach, Florida, Tae Kwon Do master Sang Koo Kang relies heavily on traditional one-step sparring for self-defense training, believing it is vital basic training for Tae Kwon Doists. "I tell students to think their one-step sparring is serious and really is a life-threatening situation. Then one-step tech-

niques become more than just a number. They become the basics for instant self-defense reactions," explains Kang.

What Is One-Step Sparring?

One-step sparring is a formula to use when attacked. The techniques include both blocks and offensive counters. If practiced every day, one-step sparring techniques become automatic defense reactions. For instance, if someone attacks you, you respond with a defensive block that redirects his power and opens a target area for your own counterattack. That is the secret of successful one-step sparring: block, find the opponent's weakness, and counterattack.

There are twenty-five different one-step sparring combinations. In Kang's school, students at each belt-rank level learn and practice five one-step sparring techniques. White to yellow belts learn one through five; orange to green belts one through ten; blue to brown belts one through fifteen; and red belts up to twenty. Finally, black belts master all twenty-five. Called "one-step" because only a single attack is allowed, one-step sparring requires two people, an attacker and a defender. From the attacker's single attacking punch, the defender draws upon any of the twenty-five prearranged techniques for his defense. Training partners trade techniques back and forth, with the attacker becoming the defender and vice versa.

The exact progression calls for the attacker to step into a ready position and utter a loud *kihap* (yell), asking for permission to attack. Next, the defender readies himself and through his own *kihap* gives the attacker permission to advance. After the consenting yell, the attacker launches a reverse punch toward the defender, who moves out of the line of fire before the punch arrives and returns the attack with a hand, foot, or combination counterattack from his group of one-step sparring techniques. No hard contact is ever made with one-step sparring.

One-step sparring's benefits become apparent in tournament sparring. Without it, many techniques lack control and form is incorrect.

Control and Contact

Besides teaching control of defensive techniques, one-step sparring teaches students of Tae Kwon Do to accept and respond to an attacking punch aimed directly at them while maintaining control of their own techniques. While some say this kind of no-contact control leads to inhibited extension and lack of power when it's needed, Kang disagrees. According to him, the kind of control that teaches fighters to stop their techniques, even at full speed and power, has nothing to do with the penetration needed for full-contact fighting. If a fighter can stop his kick or punch inches away from his opponent, he can go all the way with full power if necessary. "Martial arts techniques take a long time to master. If you cannot use control while learning and practicing them, you won't have any sparring partners," Kang says. Tournament techniques must be fully extended and clean-looking in order to score any points. From controlled one-step sparring, students learn to fully extend punches and kicks. There are no wild uncontrollable movements that lead to poorly snapped, off-center punches and sloppy kicks. One-step sparring's good clean techniques come from control and accuracy.

Accuracy

Accuracy is the next attribute of one-step sparring. Without accuracy, which comes from practicing strikes aimed directly at the target and stopped with control, punches and kicks lack focus and power. Forms training develops technically correct techniques, but it does not provide the target that teaches accuracy. Some styles of Chinese martial arts get around this by using a wooden dummy to simulate a human being. Although students learn to be accurate, they do not learn control from wooden-dummy practice. One-step sparring provides students with a target they can't hit randomly and without control.

Speed

One-step sparring also develops speed. Although one-step sparring sounds like a slow-motion series of movements, it isn't at all slow. If practiced correctly, one-step sparring techniques are done at full speed. As techniques become better defined, speed comes more easily. Tae Kwon Do also uses two- and three-step sparring (where the attacker punches two or three times before the defender can return the attack), but Kang prefers one-step sparring. The single punch forces the defender to be quick to block and respond with a counterattack. He doesn't have the extra time that results from two or three punches to draw up a plan of counterattack.

Power

One-step sparring also allows Tae Kwon Do stylists to perfect their body connection and motion to their maximum potential for speed and power. Since one-step sparring consists of a series of prearranged techniques that students practice over and over before they get into actual freestyle sparring, the proper delivery of power through the correct use of body angles and waist and hip movements becomes reflexive. When fighters put together control, speed, and correct body motion, they have natural penetrating power. To further develop power and penetration, Kang's students also practice with power against hanging bags and engage in freestyle sparring.

Simple to Sophisticated

One-step sparring techniques start simple, with a block and counter. The counter may be a kick, such as a waist-level side kick, or a hand technique, like a knife-hand to the neck. The attacker may start with a reverse punch to head or body. The attacker gets only one opportunity to attack. There is no trading back and forth of techniques. A typical one-step sparring block might be a simple redirecting outer block, followed immediately by a side kick, ax kick, or roundhouse kick. A more complicated one-step sparring technique starts with the expected reverse punch. After the block, Kang's students might counter with a reverse punch, followed by an elbow strike to the head. One-step sparring counters may have punches following kicks and kicks following punches. There are few limits to the possibilities in one-step sparring.

Jane Hallander is a veteran martial arts writer and a regular contributor to CFW Enterprises publications. This material originally appeared in the April 1994 edition of Inside Tae Kwon Do *magazine.*

7

Training for Tae Kwon Do Competition

Kathy Yeh, M.A.

A national Tae Kwon Do champion lays out a step-by-step guide for aspiring competitors, answering all these important questions: When will you train? How long will your training sessions last? How hard will you work out? What types of drills will you do? Do you need training partners?

So you've decided you want to compete. Now what? To perform your best in competition you need an effective training program. First, determine your goals and objectives. Are you planning to enter your first local tournament, or are you trying to get a place on the Tae Kwon Do National Team? If you're entering a local tournament, your program will probably not be the same as if you were trying to get on the national team.

The next step is designing your training program. This includes when, how, and with whom you'll be training. What days will you train? How long will the training sessions last? How hard will you work out? What types of drills will you do? Do you need partners to train with? It is wise to

answer some if not all of these questions before you begin.

Three Energy Systems

First, some basic information about the human body and how it adapts to training is helpful. Martial artists can draw from the field of exercise physiology to improve their training methods. There are three energy systems in the human body: the immediate, the short-term, and the aerobic. The immediate and short-term systems (anaerobic systems) are used primarily in brief, intense energy bursts like those required to deliver an explosive roundhouse kick or to repeatedly throw powerful kicks. After about two minutes of activity the aerobic system begins to contribute a greater proportion of energy.

Specificity

Training can improve the capacity of these energy systems, but only if they are stressed or overloaded in the correct manner. This is referred to as "specificity" and applies to training both the energy anaerobic and aerobic systems. Training your anaerobic systems produces an increase in the enzymes that break down glucose (the fuel your body needs for intense activity) and an increase in tolerance for lactic-acid levels in the muscles. Lactic acid is produced by intense activity and can contribute to fatigue. Research has shown that highly trained athletes can tolerate much higher levels of lactic acid than less-trained athletes. Training can also improve your mental ability to deal with fatigue and your pain tolerance. What this means for the Tae Kwon Doist is that you need to tailor your training to develop these energy systems, especially the anaerobic.

The emphasis in training should be to mimic the actual movements and skills required in competition. To increase the ability of the muscles to deliver powerful and explosive kicks, you must practice kicks. The training carry-over from other activities, like biking, is limited. Your legs will become stronger when you bike, but you aren't using the muscles the way they are used when you kick. The speed at which you practice your kicks or punches is also important. It should be the same as that needed in competition. This trains the muscles you're using to recruit and synchronize the motor units in the desired pattern.

Individualization

Another consideration in developing your training program is individualization. Every person starts at a different fitness level and will adapt to training in his or her unique way. For example, two runners may have the same training program, but one may beat the other in competition. It is also unrealistic to think that everyone is capable of doing the same techniques effectively. Just because it worked for Jimmy Kim, the Olympic gold medalist, or Lydia Zele, world Tae Kwon Do championship gold medalist, does not mean it will work for you. Each person must use those techniques that work best for his or her body. It is better to have a few good, sharp techniques that you can depend on than to have many kicks that are mediocre (although the more variety you have the more difficult an opponent you will be). Keep this in mind if you are developing a program for a student or for yourself

Training for Competition

Training for competition should begin several months before the date of the competition, in order for the body to adapt and improve. The training program should be progressive; that is, as you get in better condition the intensity, frequency, and duration of your training sessions should be adjusted. All of these do not need to be adjusted at the same time.

Intensity applies not only to the whole workout session, but can vary with different exercises and drills. One way to monitor your intensity in specific drills is to throw a specified number of techniques in a certain time period and work on increasing that number. For example, do 20 roundhouse kicks on the heavy bag in one minute, then add to that at your next workout. Intensity can also be varied by working drills at different percentages of your maximum ability. One drill can be performed at 100 percent and another at 75 percent.

Successful competitors vary greatly in the frequency and duration of their workouts. Some people may train two or three times per day, seven days per week, others once per day six days per week. This is something that you have to discover for yourself. Pay attention to how you feel both physically and mentally, and as your training progresses, adapt your program accordingly. In my experience, training six days per week for two hours is adequate for improvements and success in competition.

Be aware of overtraining. Some signs to watch for are fatigue, listlessness, lack of motivation, irritability, more frequent injury, injuries that take longer to heal, sleeplessness, elevated heart rate after working out, severe muscle cramping, and loss of speed or power. Whatever the frequency or duration of your training sessions, you need to allow your body time to rest and adapt to training. This is true both between bouts of intense activity in one training session and between training sessions. Maximum bouts of one minute should be followed by two to three minutes of rest to allow the body to recoup its energy stores.

This rest can be active, which means doing another exercise at a much lower intensity, such as stretching or walking around. Active recovery encourages a quicker recovery than passive recovery—in other words, i.e., sitting down. Easier workouts can be followed by very intense workouts.

Other Considerations

Other considerations when planning your training include variety of drills and exercises, and evaluation of your progress and techniques. Variety keeps you interested and motivated. Consistent, focused training is a challenge, so you need to keep your program exciting. Evaluation can be performed by a coach, sparring partner, and/or yourself, and gives you important feedback in areas you need to work on as well as your strong points. It is an important tool for modifying your program.

Often in training, the feedback focuses on what we are doing wrong, but there needs to be a balance of negative and positive input. Too much criticism can undermine an athlete's confidence. On the other hand, competitors should not be overconfident or have false ideas of their skill levels. Knowing when and how to give constructive feedback is an art form.

All training sessions should include warm-up, stretching, and cool-down phases. The warm-up prepares the mind and body for activity. As you warm up, your heart rate and circulation increase, delivering more blood to the working muscles. Warming up decreases the risk of muscle and joint injuries and improves your ability to perform work. Light stretching can be done after a warm-up, saving the more intense stretching for after the cool-down phase. Stretching maintains or increases the range of motion of joints and thus reduces the risk of injury. It can also decrease the soreness that may result after a workout. The cool-down allows your heart rate and circulation to gradually return to resting levels. It reduces the chance of dizziness, fainting, and the pooling of blood in your extremities.

Training Exercises

Training programs should be individualized. The following are some suggestions to help prepare you for competition and to stimulate your thinking about other drills you can do. The number of different drills is limited only by your imagination, so long as you keep in mind your ultimate goal. As you practice, think offensively as well as defensively. Imagine your opponent in front of you. Start with one minute initially, or less if you are unable to go for a full minute. As you improve, gradually increase your time to three minutes—the length of a Tae Kwon Do tournament round. Remember to include rest periods, preferably active ones, between drills. It's a good idea to wear all of your sparring equipment— headgear, mouthpiece, chest protector, arm pads, and shin guards— during your training sessions. The goal is to be comfortable in the equipment and simulate the competitive environment as much as possible.

Warming Up with a Jump Rope (Footwork Exercises)

Jumping rope is an excellent way to develop endurance needed for competition and to improve footwork. Practice different jumping techniques and patterns. Stay on the balls of your feet as you jump. Concentrate on developing a rhythm. As you improve, increase your speed, jumping more times per minute. Here are a few suggestions to get you jumping:

1. Jump rope laps around the dojang, using an easy skipping motion (just like you used to jump rope as a child).
2. Jump both feet to the right, left, right, etc., on the balls of your feet.
   Variation: As you improve, add to the exercise by taking the rope in both hands and circling it backward to the right side and forward, and then circling it backward to the left side and forward. Then return to the basics.
3. Jump bringing your knees high toward your chest.

While it is important to have dynamic, strong techniques, this alone will not allow you to score. Good footwork is what will get you in a position to hit your opponent and also avoid getting hit. These exercises will improve your footwork:

1. Stepping forward: With your left leg in front, move your right foot up to the left foot and slide your left foot forward. Practice moving quickly and smoothly.
2. Stepping backward: With your left leg in front, step back with your right foot, followed by your left foot (stopping where your right foot was).

Practice 10 times on each side. Repeat exercises, adding a kick or combination of kicks after you have stepped.

Sparring

Spar often and with as many skilled partners as possible—ideally, partners of your same weight category and gender. Sparring develops your fighting techniques as well as your fighting strategy. This is where you put your techniques together in an effective manner, responding to your partner. Work on balancing control and your partner's safety with being able to throw your techniques with as much power as possible. Practice in the same size area as the official Tae Kwon Do competitive ring, 12 meters by 12 meters.

Using Focus Mitts, Body Bags, or Heavy Bags

Doing drills using focus mitts can help develop speed, focus, and timing. In order to develop the reach of your kicks, stay as far away as you can from the mitt and your partner while still being able to reach them. The advantage of working with body bags or heavy bags is that when you work with a sparring partner or practice drills with no striking surface, you rarely use all your power. When you work with body bags or heavy bags, you can work at 100 percent of your strength. This stresses the muscles involved in the technique and further develops strength. You can also move in closer to the bags to practice your inside fighting techniques.

1. **Double roundhouse kick**: Assume a left-leg-lead fighting stance. Throw a roundhouse with your back (right) leg, set your right foot down next to your left foot, step back quickly with your left leg, and throw a left-leg roundhouse. Concentrate on power and a quick transition step between kicks. Repeat 10 times, switch stance, and perform 10 repetitions on the other side.
   Variation: Throw the first kick high and the second kick low, or vice versa.

2. **Turn-back kick/roundhouse kick combination**: Assume a left-leg-lead fighting stance. Throw a right-leg turn back kick. Follow up with a back-leg roundhouse with the left leg. Repeat 10 times and switch to the other side.

   Variation: Roundhouse kick/turn-back kick combination. With your left leg forward, throw a right-leg roundhouse, follow with a left-leg turn-back kick. Do 10 times on each side.

3. **Roundhouse kick/hook kick combination**: Assume a left-leg-lead fighting stance. Throw a right-leg roundhouse followed by a left-leg spinning hook kick. Repeat 10 times and switch to the other side.

4. **Ax kick/roundhouse kick combination**: Your partner should hold the focus mitt at a 45-degree angle to the ground (about head level of the person who is kicking) for the ax kick, and change the position of the mitt for the roundhouse kick so that the flat surface is almost vertical to the ground. Assume a left-leg-lead fighting stance. Bring your right foot up to your left foot and throw a left-leg ax kick followed by a right back-leg roundhouse. Your partner should step back for the roundhouse kick. Repeat 10 times on each side, performing the kicks as fast as you can with good technique.

5. **Back-leg/front-leg roundhouse kick combination**: Assume a left-leg-lead fighting position. Throw a back-leg roundhouse with your right leg, either to the torso or to the head. Set your right leg down in front, followed with a high roundhouse with the same leg. Don't change your foot position on the second kick, just pop it up to the head. If your partner is holding a mitt he or she may need to step back after the first kick. Repeat 10 times and switch to the other side.

6. **Side kick/roundhouse kick double kick**: Both people assume a fighting stance with opposite lead legs. One person throws a front-leg side kick, rechambers the leg and throws a high roundhouse. Repeat 10 times and switch sides.

7. **Back-leg roundhouse kick/counter-turn back kick**: Both people assume a fighting stance with opposite lead legs. One person throws a back-leg roundhouse kick, the other counters with a turn back kick. Repeat 10 times on each side.

8. **Ax kick/counter turn-back kick**: Both people assume a fighting stance with the same leg forward. One person throws a back-leg ax kick, the other counters with a turn-back kick. Repeat 10 times on each side.

9. **"Flash" the mitt**: Imagine that you are sparring as you do this drill. Your partner should move around the ring as he "flashes" the focus mitt out in different angles and positions. You can do this with two focus mitts as well. The person kicking hits the target as fast as he can with an appropriate technique; this depends on how the mitt is positioned. Don't hold or leave the target out.

10. **Rounds**: Work on timed rounds, using any technique you want, with the body bag or the heavy bag. During the rest period between rounds, you can do abdominal exercises or stretch. Focus on speed and strength while visualizing an opponent. Start with 3 rounds and work up.

11. **"Torture drill"**: A favorite of Debbie Pedersen, coach of national and international Tae Kwon Do champions, this drill develops speed, footwork, and quick reflexes. The person holding the focus mitts has one in each hand, with the flat surface perpendicular to the floor. The person kicking throws four back-leg roundhouses moving forward and four back-leg roundhouses moving backward, alternating legs. Four kicks forward and four kicks backward is one set. The goal

is to perform 4 sets in a row, but you may want to start with fewer sets.

Start with the right leg in front, throw a left back-leg roundhouse moving forward and set the left leg down in front. Continue by throwing a back-leg roundhouse with the right leg, again setting the kicking leg down in front. As you complete the fourth round-house with your right leg, set the right leg down in front. Immediately, and without changing foot position, throw a left-leg roundhouse with the back leg. Set the left foot down directly in front and right next to your right foot, and then step back with your right foot. Continue by throwing a right back-leg roundhouse and stepping back-ward in the same way, until you have com-pleted four kicks going backward. As you throw the fourth back-leg roundhouse kick with your right leg, set the foot down and step back. Continue by going through the same sequence as in the beginning of the drill, until you have completed 4 sets.

Conclusion

The development of a training program is a very individualized process. The most effective program is one designed to meet your specific goals and to evolve and change as you do. Training develops and forms the foundation of your fighting skills, but experience, motivation, and courage will also deter-mine your success in competition.

Kathy Yeh has been training in Tae Kwon Do for more than fifteen years, and has competed successfully in both open-style and Tae Kwon Do tournaments. A bronze medalist at the Tae Kwon Do Nationals and the Olympic Festival in 1991, she lives in Oakland, California, and works for a major corporation as a health and fitness specialist. This material originally appeared in the January 1996 issue of Inside Tae Kwon Do *magazine.*

8

Your Ultimate Stretching Guide

Andre Alex Lima

The good news is, deep inside, we all know that someday soon we'll be kickin' just like Bill "Superfoot" Wallace or Bruce Lee. The bad news is, deep inside, we know we need just a little work on our flexibility before achieving greatness. The good news is, stretching expert Andre Lima is going to help us "surpass our limitations!" The bad news is, he smiles when he says it.

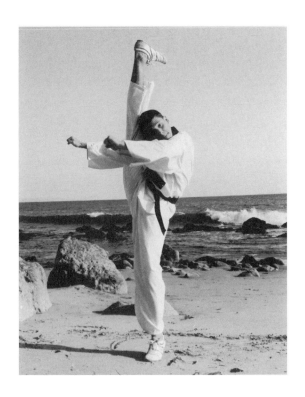

Today just about everybody in the martial arts wants to perform flamboyant splits and fancy kicks. Kicks are always in fashion, and are among the most popular techniques in the martial arts. Tae Kwon Do is the martial art that makes the most use of them. But in order to perform these kicks, you must be flexible. If you are not so flexible, but nevertheless aspire to acquire those flashy kicks, be confident—you still can! You'll need to work very hard on your stretching to reach your goal. And you'll need help. This chapter will show you how to do it the right way.

First of all, to achieve your kicking goals you must know your own limitations. Then, armed with a well-directed and progressive training program, you will surpass those limitations. You need to change the way you think about stretching. Adopting a new attitude will help you save time in reaching your goals and avoid the stretching injuries so common to martial artists. Beginners, who typically try to behave and/or perform like champions prematurely, often become frustrated and lose motivation if the results don't come as fast as they expect. Remember, even the late, great Bruce Lee had to stretch a lot to do all those great kicks of his.

To form your goals in flexibility, you must consider essential factors such as your age, gender, weight, genetics, physical condition, mental condition, and other personal details that will be explained later. This chapter will explain, based on scientific experiments, how much your general performance—in Tae Kwon Do and in all sports—will improve as your flexibility does. Get ready to enter a whole new world that will stretch your body and your imagination.

What Is Stretching, and Why Should You Do It?

Stretching, very simply, is a progressive system of exercise that increases the flexibility of muscles, joints, and connective tissue—that is, their ability to move through their full range of motion. Martial artists in general should want to improve their flexibility through stretching exercises. Among other things, stretching can:

- optimize the learning, practice, and performance of many types of skilled movements
- increase mental and physical relaxation
- promote body awareness development
- reduce risk of joint sprain or muscle strain, muscular tension and soreness, and the severity of painful menstruation for female athletes

To begin with, it should be understood that stretching is indeed a form of exercise. Although generally referred to in a passive sense, stretching can be conducted in a number of ways, one of which uses isometric contraction of the muscle in question to improve flexibility and range of motion. Even in the passive sense, where the range of motion is slowly being increased, the muscle fibers are resisting the movement to a certain extent and adapting to the increased range.

Although the main focus of stretching is usually the muscle tissue itself, the joints and connective tissue (ligaments, tendons, and cartilage) can benefit to some degree as well. Stretching helps to warm up the tissue of the body, causing a slight rise in temperature and signaling the release of lubrication fluids from the sacs within each joint. Obviously, muscle tissue receives the greater benefit; stretching enhances its flexibility and, therefore, its ability to contract more effectively and safely.

An essential point concerning stretching is that its benefits are progressive. In other words, the more you stretch, the better you will become at it. Then, once you have reached a certain degree of flexibility, predicated to an extent on your genetics, you can maintain this level easily and still get terrific benefits including making your Tae Kwon Do technique more efficient.

More importantly, flexible muscles are more resistant to strains and tears. Safety, in fact, is one of the crucial reasons for stretching out. Stretching not only ameliorates tissue flexibility; it arouses blood flow into the muscles in question as well. A few minutes spent completing these motions prior to any of your martial art training sessions will prevent injuries and help you reach your workout goals.

Now that you have a basic understanding of what is meant by the word stretching, you can realize how well it fits into your Tae Kwon Do training: it makes muscles resistant to injuries that can occur due to sudden stresses, plus makes them contract better and more quickly. Always prepare your body before diving into more stressful and energizing movements.

Stretch before you work out, but also use the same motions to help your body warm down after you are finished. This will help reduce muscle soreness and speed the removal of lactic acid and other metabolic wastes from the tissues, making you recover much sooner. In addition, a good number of stretches can and should be executed while you are exercising, so as to maximize muscle and nerve function and make your training more efficient.

Finally, it must be stated that stretching is actually enhanced when conducted after a short warm-up of another type. Five minutes on an exercise bike at a light intensity, or a half-mile walk to the gym or the martial art school, gets the blood flow started and forces the body temperature to rise. This in turn makes the muscles more supple to begin with and, therefore, more able to benefit from a stretching regimen.

You must warm up your body more thoroughly before embarking on advanced stretching exercises. The series of exercises we'll be showing you systematically loosens and gently stretches all of the important muscle groups in your body. By spending fifteen minutes on these warm-ups, your body will be prepared for the more demanding stretching exercises that follow, and you will be able to exert more pressure on muscles, tendons, and ligaments without causing injuries.

A Note on Body Mechanics

Prior to proceeding there is some information that we should consider. Each muscle is either an *adductor* or an *abductor*. Adductor muscles bring the body back to normal alignment; abductor muscles pull the bones away from the body. For example, the quadriceps, which pulls the leg out, is an abductor muscle; the sartorius, which pulls the leg back in, is an adductor muscle. Note that muscles always pull a bone; they never push. In any movement muscles work in pairs. One muscle acts as an *agonist*, while an opposing muscle acts as an *antagonist*. The agonist muscle pulls to make the necessary movement. The antagonist muscle must relax and stretch, otherwise it

works against the agonist. For example, in the moment you execute a front kick, the quadriceps do the work, and are thus the agonist; the biceps femoris are, in this case, the antagonist.

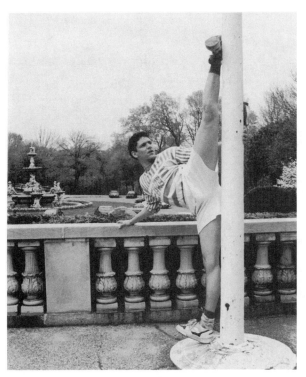

Anywhere is a good place for stretching. Therefore, don't make excuses! Change your attitude and enjoy the experience.

Progressive Stretching and Tae Kwon Do

Good flexibility allows a Tae Kwon Doist to perform a higher kick with longer reach and less effort, and, consequently, with less energy waste and greater technical effectiveness. With poor flexibility, Tae Kwon Doists will have less balance when they try to perform a high kick. And, without good flexibility to perform a high kick with balance, imagine how difficult it will be to accomplish a sequence of high kicks during a contest or a fight.

Following a progressive Tae Kwon Do training program means two things: one, attempting to increase the body's range of motion for each stretch every time it is done; and two, starting by working the larger muscles and moving down the line to smaller ones. This ensures that the body will be completely warmed up and stretched out before you begin your martial arts workout, which will help prevent injuries and maximize the benefits of every workout.

Remember, post-training stretching is also critical. Warming down the body is essential to speeding recovery, which, in turn, translates into greater muscle and connective tissue strength and lessened muscle soreness.

Stretching Methods

A number of different stretching methods can improve your flexibility. All of these require proper form, careful attention to detail and to the sensations you are experiencing, and some exercise smarts. If you stretch out with proper form, you will certainly reap numerous benefits. However, as with all exercise, if you are sloppy or haphazard in your stretching you will probably hurt more than help yourself.

To get the most out of the exercises and to prevent injuries, pay attention to the exercise you are doing, keeping the movement totally concentrated

Side kick split with a partner

on the muscle you are working for maximum development. And learn to keep your mental attitude positive.

Stretching exercises are performed in a variety of ways depending upon your goals, abilities, and state of training. For example, a world-class gymnast or black belt in Tae Kwon Do should perform more advanced stretches than individuals who are beginning stretching programs simply to improve their personal health and fitness.

There are five basic stretching techniques: static, dynamic, passive, active, and proprioceptive. Let's examine each of them.

Static Stretching

Static stretching involves holding a position. That is, you stretch to the farthest possible point and hold the stretch. Splits are a good example of this kind of stretching. The most important advantage of static stretching is that it is the safest method of stretching. Other advantages include these:

- It requires little expenditure of energy.
- It allows adequate time to reset the sensitivity of the stretch reflex.*
- It permits semipermanent change in length.
- It can induce muscular relaxation if the stretch is held long enough.

Dynamic Stretching

Dynamic stretching involves bobbing, bouncing, rebounding, and rhythmic types of movements. This technique is the most controversial stretching method because it can cause the most soreness and injury. Other disadvantages are these:

*The stretch reflex, initiated whenever a muscle is stretched, is a basic operation of the nervous system that helps maintain muscle tone and prevent injury. Stretching a muscle lengthens both the muscle fibers and the muscle spindles—encapsulated structures that run parallel to the muscle fibers. The lengthening of the muscle spindles results in the firing of the stretch reflex: the muscle that is being stretched contracts. The reflex diminishes as you hold a stretch, allowing the muscles to relax and lengthen further.

- It fails to provide adequate time for the tissues to adapt to the stretch.
- It initiates the stretch reflex and thereby increases muscular tension, making it more difficult to stretch out the connective tissues.
- It does not provide adequate time for neurological adaptation (i.e., of the stretch reflex) to take place.

Despite these disadvantages, there are several reasons why some athletes might use dynamic stretching exercises. This method is effective for developing flexibility. More importantly, in terms of specificity of training it is appropriate for developing dynamic flexibility (movement due to momentum). This is essential for certain events and sports, such as ballet and Tae Kwon Do. Subjectively, dynamic stretching can be less boring than other stretching methods.

Passive (or Partner-Assisted) Stretching

Passive stretching is a technique in which you relax and make no contribution to the range of motion. Instead, an external force, either a partner or a machine, does the work. Among the advantages associated with passive stretching are these:

- It is effective when the agonist (the primary muscle responsible for the movement) is too weak to respond.
- It is effective when attempts to inhibit the tight muscles (the antagonists, which will respond with the stretch reflex) are unsuccessful.
- It allows stretching beyond one's active range of motion.
- Direction, duration, and intensity can be measured when more advanced stretching machines and modalities are used in rehabilitative therapy.
- It can promote team comradeship when athletes stretch with partners.

The major disadvantage associated with passive stretching is its greater risk of soreness and injury if a partner applies the external force incorrectly. If the stretch is too rapid, it may initiate the stretch reflex and the likelihood of injury increases with greater differences between the ranges of active and passive flexibility. But the solution here is to also develop your active flexibility.

As long as the two of you communicate, neither will be injured, and both will benefit greatly from working in tandem. You will find your flexibility enhanced tremendously through partner assistance. Further, some of these drills simply cannot be done alone, such as shoulder stretches, where your arms are pulled behind your back and lifted.

Ax kick split with a partner

Any of these stretching techniques can be done with the help of another person. In fact, stretching in this manner may be more beneficial simply because a partner can help coax you to stretch beyond the range of motion you would attempt on your own.

Active and Active Isolated Stretching

Active stretching is accomplished using your own muscles without any assistance. An example of active stretching is standing upright and slowly lifting one leg to a 45-degree angle. Active stretching is important because it develops active flexibility, which has a higher correlation with sports achievement than does passive flexibility.

The major disadvantages of active stretching are that it may initiate the stretch reflex and it may be ineffective in the presence of certain dysfunction and injuries such as severe sprains, inflammation, or fractures.

The newest area of flexibility study concerns AI, or "active isolated" stretching. AI involves the contraction of one muscle to stretch its antagonist. An example would be the tight flexing of the quadriceps to stretch the hamstrings, and vice versa. The contraction is held only for two to three seconds, after which the muscle is relaxed for the same length of time. This two-step approach is repeated up to eight times, the participant exhaling with each contractile stretch. This method of gaining flexibility can be used by itself or, for best results, accompanying standard static stretching.

Proprioceptive Neuromuscular Facilitation (PNF)

Proprioceptive neuromuscular facilitation (PNF) is another broad strategy that can improve your range of motion. This technique is also referred to in certain disciplines as a muscle energy technique. PNF was originally designed and developed as a physical therapy procedure for rehabilitation. Today, several different types of PNF are being used in sports medicine. Two of the most prevalent are the contract-relax technique and the contract-relax-contract technique.

Contract-Relax Technique (Hold-Relax)

This technique starts with the athlete's tight muscle group in a lengthened position. Assume for the sake of illustration that your hamstrings are tight. The tight hamstrings are first placed under a gentle stretch and then gradually contracted isometrically, building to a maximum effort for 6 to 15 seconds against the resistance of your partner. There is no change in the muscle's length or movement of the joint. This is followed by a brief period of relaxing the hamstrings. Then your partner slowly lengthens the tight muscle group by passively moving the extremity through its gained range of motion.

Contract-Relax-Contract Technique (Hold-Relax-Contract)

This technique is similar to the contract-relax one except that after the relaxation phase you actively contract the agonist (that is, the antagonist of the tight muscle group, which in this instance is your quadriceps). This last phase can also be assisted by the partner. Then the entire procedure is repeated.

PNF techniques are claimed to offer a wider range of advantages and benefits than conventional stretching methods. Most significantly, PNF is claimed to be the most successful method for developing flexibility. It is also praised because it enhances active flexibility and helps establish a pattern for coordinated motion. It is also considered superior because it uses several important neurophysiological mechanisms (including such things as reciprocal innervation and the inverse myotatic reflex). For example, PNF techniques may help reset the stretch reflex level, promoting relaxation in the muscles to be stretched.

Unfortunately, PNF techniques have several disadvantages. Most important is the greater risk of injury, ranging from a pulled muscle to certain cardiovascular complications. Furthermore, this technique requires a knowledgeable and well-trained partner.

Specific Stretching for Tae Kwon Do

By now you should realize that stretching programs vary from workout to workout and sport to sport and should be tailored to your needs. Different activities have varying stresses on the body that must be addressed specifically. In other words, if you are going to throw kicks on a heavy bag, you need to practice different stretches than you would if you were set to throw punches on that same bag.

Many of the flexibility movements overlap from one activity to the next, but others are more specific. No matter what you are going to do, always begin with a brief warm-up. Tae Kwon Do fighters relying on high kicks or other combat techniques should particularly spend time on dynamic stretching of their legs. Starting slowly, they should gradually raise their legs higher. Later, they should increase the speed of the movements even using the "hand-kicking" drill.

A good example of dynamic stretching regularly practiced in Tae Kwon Do classes is the front stretching kick, which consists of raising the leg up as high as possible with the knee straight. This type of training is excellent for Tae Kwon Do. Static stretching is the other method of training that best fits Tae Kwon Do programs because of its many advantages: safety, little expenditure of energy, and the ability to induce muscular relaxation. A good example of this type of stretching is the splits.

Final Tips: How to Choose the Right Exercises

The kind of martial art you practice will determine the kind of stretching exercises you should perform. If you are a Tae Kwon Do student, the majority of strokes you do are with your feet, so you should choose a greater variety of stretching exercises for your legs. A kickboxer, however, uses mostly the arms, shoulders, and neck; therefore, he or she should choose a richer variety of upper-body stretching exercises.

Stretching for Younger Students

Normally, children don't need to dedicate as much time to flexibility improvement as adults do. Their bodies are much more elastic. Five to ten minutes of stretching exercises per workout is enough. In children, excitation dominates over inhibition in the nervous system. This means that it is hard for a child to stay in the same place and relax or concentrate in static stretching. Therefore, the best method for children may be dynamic stretching, using exercises with a full range of motion.

Age eight to eleven for girls and ten to thirteen for boys is the right time to intensify their flexibility training; at this age they will start gaining mass faster than height and will probably reduce their range of motion. In the second stage of adolescence, at age thirteen to fifteen for girls and fifteen to nineteen for boys, flexibility training can once again be intensified, this time with sport-specific stretches, until they reach the same level as adults.

Flexibility and the Older Student

Flexibility can be developed at any age given the appropriate training. However, the rate of development will not be the same at every age for all athletes. Generally speaking, small children are quite supple, and flexibility increases during the school years. With the onset of adolescence, flexibility tends to level off, and then begins to decrease through adulthood. The decline in flexibility with age is brought on by changes that occur in the connective tissues of the body. It has been suggested that exercise can delay the loss of flexibility due to the aging process. This is based on the notion that exercise, including stretching, stimulates the production or retention of lubricants between the connective tissue fibers.

Stretching for Beginners

Your level of conditioning will affect how much flexibility training you include, but the basics should be practiced by everyone. Anyone just getting started with Tae Kwon Do, any other kind of martial art, or even any new sporting activity should be especially committed to warming up and stretching. Nothing is more potentially damaging to muscle tissue than the stress of actions it is not accustomed to or prepared for. Even if your muscles oblige you by performing the necessary action, they will haunt you later with incredible soreness. Because of its preparatory function, stretching reduces the chance of injury, enhances muscular coordination and function, cuts down on after-workout soreness, and helps you to perform more effectively, especially when you are a beginner.

Weight Lifting and Flexibility

Weight lifting makes muscle fiber thicker and shorter; flexibility training makes it thinner and longer. However, you cannot say that weight lifting is bad for flexibility. Once you organize yourself well enough to do both workouts in equal proportion, you will be able to have big, strong muscles and also be very flexible. The mistake a lot of people make is to lift weights and neglect to stretch their muscles properly.

Speed and Flexibility

If you are not very flexible and try to fire several kicks at your opponent's face, you will expend a lot of energy because your muscle will have considerable resistance to the movement. Then, you will obviously lose speed. On the other hand, if you are flexible, your muscles will not have resistance when you are kicking. You will spend a lot less energy and you will be able to get good speed and be a fast kicker. Will you kick like Bill "Superfoot" Wallace? Well, maybe, with a few years of steady practice. Good luck!

STRETCHING TIPS

1. Always make sure safety comes first in order to prevent any injury.

2. Identify specific and realistic goals.

3. Do not stretch immediately before eating.

4. Discard all candy, gum, or any kind of food during stretching.

5. Wear loose and comfortable clothes.

6. Remove all jewelry.

7. Select a clean and quiet place to stretch.

8. Work on a nonskid surface, preferably a firm mat.

9. Avoid stretching in places that are too cold.

10. Warm up prior to stretching.

11. Develop a positive mental attitude.

12. Isolate the muscle group to be stretched.

13. Move slowly and smoothly into the stretch to avoid initiation of the stretch reflex.

14. Use proper biomechanics and strive for correct alignment.

15. Breathe normally and freely, but accentuate the exhalation when moving deeper into the stretch.

16. Hold the stretch (usually about 20 to 60 seconds) and relax. Do not strain or passively force a joint beyond its normal range of motion.

17. Concentrate and feel the stretch.

18. Anticipate and communicate when stretching with a partner.

19. Come out of each stretch as carefully as you went into it.

20. Try to understand what you are doing; information helps a lot.

21. Be persistent. Do not give up so easily. The results will come with time.

22. Have fun!

Andre Alex Lima of Venice, California, is a retired European Tae Kwon Do heavyweight champion and one of the world's leading martial arts freelance writers. His articles have appeared in martial arts magazines throughout the world in various languages. This material originally appeared in the May and June 1995 issues of Inside Tae Kwon Do *magazine.*

9

Championship Kicking
Four Exercises to Help You Get a Leg Up on the Competition

Andrew Breen

On a purely technical level, the knee plays an integral role in the execution of kicks. But its importance is often neglected or overlooked. Here, the author shows you how superior chambering can help you get a leg up on the competition.

What is the most discouraging aspect of trying to kick an opponent and coming up short? Are your kicks consistently jammed before the kick is even underway? Do you constantly experience the unenviable feeling of being maneuvered into such an uncomfortable range that you do not have room to kick? Or is it just that your kicks lack the sharp stopping power needed to keep an opponent honest?

Fortunately, you can alleviate these problems with a simple, yet effective intervention: namely, improving the lifting and chambering motion of the knee. Of course, other components are necessary to landing one's kicks consistently. Timing, footwork, and strategy are all essential ingredients in the mix. Nonetheless, on a purely mechanical level, nothing is as important as acquiring the habit of raising the knee as high as possible and coiling it tightly prior to kick-

ing. This should be complemented by retracting the leg in a similarly controlled manner.

The knee plays a critical role for several reasons. First, the knee acts as a hinge to transmit the power of a kick. Pointing the knee in the direction of the target enlists the mass of the hips and lower body by providing a straight line of force from the hips to the lower leg.

The High Knee Chamber

Second, the elevation of the knee also determines the height of the kick. A practitioner cannot deliver a potent high kick without first cranking the knee as high, or nearly as high, as the intended target. Strictly speaking, a martial artist can still kick high by dropping the knee and shoveling the lower leg up to the target. However, this method lacks power. It also requires the kicker's body to lean away precariously, thereby jeopardizing his or her balance.

A high knee chamber enables a kick to travel over the opponent's leg. This is especially helpful in clashes or against an adversary who consistently tries to jam your attack. The lower leg clears the interference set up by the opponent, who, instead of smothering the kick, is blasted by its full power. The high chamber also makes it harder for an opponent to predict where you will target the kick. One prominent example of this deceptiveness is the kicking style of Bill "Superfoot" Wallace. Wallace has said that one of the keys to his spectacular success was the fact that he would position his knee in such a manner that he could shoot out either a hook kick, side kick, or roundhouse—merely by altering the trajectory of the lower leg. Even if your kicking style is not comparable to Wallace's, the same principle applies: the higher you raise the knee, the more options you open up, and the harder it is for an opponent to block your leg.

Folding the Knee

Third, folding the knee sharply into the chest also creates extra room to kick—even at deceptively close range. Take a defensive side kick as an example. From a range of only two to three feet, the side kick unfolds like an accordion. The kick may appear too close to be practical; however, the close proximity is not a handicap but an advantage, allowing the leg to blast right through the target. Rather than being stifled, the kick explodes from a tightly coiled chamber.

In the case of a defensive hook kick, an individual can stand literally shoulder to shoulder with an opponent yet still retain the capability to kick him in the head. By lifting one's knee over the opponent's guard, the lower leg is positioned to rise over the shoulder. Another advantage is that it is difficult to see. It bypasses the opponent's normal line of vision

and is right on target before he recognizes what is happening.

Appreciating just how vital the positioning of the knee is to successful kicking, how can a martial artist put these principles into practice? The following exercises will help develop flexibility, hip strength, and endurance to make a high knee chamber a natural part of your kicking style. Many types of stretching exercises are useful for reducing the muscular tension involved. That said, flexibility is, in and of itself, insufficient to guarantee optimal height. In addition to flexibility, the hips, buttocks, and abdomen must be strengthened. One of the best ways to achieve these results is through slow motion, dynamic tension exercises. This type of training simultaneously stretches and strengthens the muscles and reinforces the habit of lifting and chambering the knee in an exaggerated fashion.

Exercise 1: Front Knee Lift Against Wall

This is one of the simplest and most effective exercises for strengthening the hips. It is also an endurance exercise par excellence. Stand facing a wall with your feet approximately two to three feet away. Place your hands against the wall at shoulder level with the upper body tilted forward slightly. From this position, alternately raise each knee to your chest. The knee should be fully flexed with each repetition and you should visualize knocking an object off your shoulder with the top of the knee. A somewhat more difficult variation involves lifting the knee to the outside.

Along with added endurance and an increased range of motion, the goal is to increase the speed and explosiveness of the initial phase of the kick, especially the front kick. Since the knee lifting exercise is designed to enhance your speed as well as your endurance, it should be done at regular speed rather than in slow motion.

Suggested routine: 3 sets of 35 to 50 repetitions.

Exercise 2: Static Knee Raise

This exercise is performed exactly as its name would indicate. Resting one hand lightly on a wall to maintain balance, raise the knee as high as possible to a roundhouse or side-kick chamber. The upper body will lean away to facilitate the lifting of the knee while the supporting leg pivots accordingly. Keep the lower leg tightly folded and place your free hand around the raised knee. Using the leverage of the arm, pull the knee up even higher. Once the knee and lower leg are at their highest point, maintain that optimal position for 15 to 30 seconds. Rest and repeat. Once you become comfortable with this exercise, you can gradually lessen your dependence on the support of the wall, eliminating it entirely if you so desire.

The static knee raise does not work particularly well when the knee is lifted to the front. However, it is extremely productive for increasing the elevation for both the side kick and the roundhouse. Although the standing leg's degree of pivot is dependent upon individual kicking style, the foot should be turned at least three quarters of the way in order to ensure proper body alignment as well as to reinforce the habit of leaning into the kick. This exercise is primarily a range of motion movement, increasing hip and adductor flexibility by using the hand to power the knee up.

Suggested routine: 2 sets of 10 repetitions.

Exercise 3: Kick Lockouts

This drill is a step up in difficulty from the previous exercise. Again, using the wall for support, slowly lift the knee into a tight side-kick or roundhouse chamber. After raising the knee, freeze it in the chambered position for two to three seconds—without the assistance of the free hand. Slowly extend the lower leg and pivot the supporting leg until the kick is at full extension. Hold that position for at least 2 to 3 seconds and then reverse the process,

retracting the leg in the same methodical manner. The aim is to deliver the kick as a three-part sequence of lifting, extending, and retracting the leg—without lowering the knee at any point. In order to maintain a high knee lift, a medium-height chair is placed approximately two feet in front of the kicking leg. The chair serves as a pointed and ever-present reminder against dropping the leg.

Each repetition should require at least 7 to 10 seconds to complete. Performed correctly and consistently, the movement develops tremendous strength in the hips and sharpens the overall execution of the side and roundhouse kicks. However, if you are not accustomed to slow-motion kicking, it is likely that this drill will initially cause cramping in the hips. The good news is that this is only temporary; improvement comes rapidly.

Suggested routine: 2 sets of 12 to 15 repetitions with each leg.

Exercise 4: Straight Line Kicking Over a Staff

This drill integrates the endurance, flexibility, and strengthening components developed by the previous three exercises. Begin by having a partner hold one end of a long stick such as a staff or broomstick with one end in front of your lower leg. The end of the staff should be held at a level somewhere between your mid-calf and lower thigh. The tip of the staff should be no more than six to eight inches away from your leg. Now, without stepping or shuffling the feet, lift and shoot a side kick over the staff—following the line of the stick as a pathway. Obviously, with the stick this close, you must draw the knee up and into the chest if you intend to clear the obstacle. The stick also motivates you to rechamber fully rather than dropping the leg straight down after lockout.

This is perhaps the toughest of the exercises, as every facet of your kicking skill is tested. There is no wall to assist you in maintaining your balance. In addition, the placement of the stick demands that you deliver—and recover—the kick with perfect form. The angle of the stick makes this an ideal exercise for the defensive side kick in that it develops the potential to fire off a powerful, penetrating side kick from close range. The tip of the stick simulates the opponent's front leg. Rather than finding yourself too jammed up to kick, you will possess the ability to draw the knee up and deliver the side kick over the interference of your opponent's front leg.

You can perform this drill slowly or at regular speed for greater realism. You can also work on your timing by modifying the exercise. Instead of simply holding the stick, have your partner thrust it into the position described earlier. When you see the stick start to move, initiate the kick so that your leg extends through the imaginary target just as the staff arrives at its stop point. You can imagine the approaching stick is a charging opponent as you fire out the kick and return to position in one smooth motion.

Suggested routine: 2 sets of 15 to 20 repetitions.

Since each drill deals with one or more of the vital components of superior chambering, the four exercises together complement each other and provide a martial artist with an excellent starting point for improving the efficacy of his or her kicks. This extra effort need not come at the expense of your regular routine. In fact, the special attention devoted to chambering ability is more productive if done on your off days, as a supplement rather than an addition to an intense workout. Attempting these demanding movements after completing a tortuous kicking session is, in fact, counterproductive. Fatigue will inhibit all that you are trying to accomplish. These exercises are best done while you are fresh and enthusiastic—after a suitable warm-up, of course.

When you consider the benefits, it's really a modest price to pay. By investing 15 minutes of well-directed effort two to three times per week, and by concentrating on this neglected aspect of the kicking process, you can begin to realize your kicking potential—both in form and function. And that may just be too good a deal to pass up.

Andrew Breen is a Boston, Massachusetts—based black belt and one of the world's finest technical martial arts writers. This material originally appeared in the August 1995 issue of Inside Tae Kwon Do *magazine.*

10

The Equipment and Training Techniques of Tae Kwon Do Master Hee Il Cho

Scott Shaw

Tae Kwon Do Master Hee Il Cho has graced the covers of more martial arts magazines than any other Tae Kwon Do stylist in history. This is in no small part due to the balletlike quality and artistic precision he portrays when delivering some of the most elaborate and difficult kicks in Tae Kwon Do's kicking arsenal. Here he discusses the innovative methods and equipment he uses in his personal training.

Master Hee Il Cho, through personal experience, knows how important proper training equipment is in the development of all offensive and defensive martial arts techniques. He remembers that back during his days as a young Tae Kwon Do stylist, the only equipment available for kicking and punching practice was duffel bags filled with sand and, in some cases, a combination of sand and sawdust. These duffel bags were suspended in the air and powerfully struck.

The problem that arose with this early training equipment, remembers Cho, was that these duffel bags would often get waterlogged from the rain, making their fillings very dense. Striking this kind of bag was like kicking or punching cement. Many early Tae Kwon Do students, in fact, sustained unnecessary injuries from striking these bags. Master Cho began studying, redesigning, and improving the way

Tae Kwon Do stylists use training equipment. He became one of the first Tae Kwon Do masters to use equipment in a truly scientific fashion to develop and enhance the various techniques of his students—as opposed to producing only sporadic improvement in their techniques or causing unforeseen injury.

Master Cho explains, "Martial artists have never really approached training and fighting as a science. There is big money involved in boxing. So boxers approach fighting from a very scientific level—how they can move better, how they can hit harder. But martial artists were just trained from master to master, generation to generation. They were all just told this technique will work, but never told *why*. Martial arts is still in a very primitive stage. Boxers know how many minutes they should jump rope, how many minutes to hit the bag, how many minutes to run. Martial artists, for the most part, don't. Now, at least, Tae Kwon Do is involved with the Olympics and they are approaching the art from a very scientific standpoint—how to kick faster, how to move faster. I have always believed in scientific training."

Kicking Bag Efficiency

With scientific knowledge as a guideline, the suspended kicking bag was the first piece of equipment Master Cho came to use in a highly efficient way. "The kicking bag is one of the most motivational tools a Tae Kwon Do student can use," states Cho. "If a student simply kicks at the air all the time, he becomes bored very fast. Kicking at a bag not only makes a big slapping sound, but the student can see the impact of his kick. This makes him understand his kicks possess power and he is learning how to defend himself successfully."

In his development of bag training, Cho first veered away from the heavy bags that weigh in at 80 to 100 pounds, which were the mainstay of the martial arts community in the 1960s and 1970s. Though he maintains that heavy bags are beneficial for practicing very specific techniques, he believes that, due to their weight, they possess the potential for unnecessary student injury when used incorrectly. "If people believe kicking a heavy bag is the best, then why don't they go and kick a cement wall?" Cho jokes. "If you constantly train on a heavy bag, and punch or kick it with full power, you will only hurt your body. And, that's not going to do anything for you." Cho drew from his personal experience in the development of his bag training. "When I came to this country [IN 1968] there were only a few companies that made bags. All they thought about was the heavy bags. Because I did a lot of spinning and jumping kicks, I could not do full-impact kicks on them because the knee cannot take that type of impact."

From this understanding, Cho designed and ordered one of the first 40-pound bags in existence and used it as a primary training tool. Today, Master

Cho focuses on training his students with lighter bags. "The kicking bag weight must be proportionate to the individual's weight," warns Cho. "A person who weighs a hundred pounds should not kick a hundred-pound bag." In Master Cho's martial arts studio in West Los Angeles, California, he has four bags of different weights. "Most people enjoy kicking the lighter bags," he says. "It is more like the feel of kicking a real person."

Master Cho himself trains daily on a 45-pound bag. He believes this is the ideal weight for a Tae Kwon Do practitioner weighing between 100 and 200 pounds. The training bag he suggests is suspended on a chain from the ceiling and is approximately 36 inches long by roughly 42 inches thick. A bag of this size allows the martial art technician to remain free of knee or joint injury, as this bag's weight will not unnaturally impact the joints of the human body. Consequently, students can make full impact with all of their techniques, thus correctly simulating opponent contact.

Cho believes the training bag is one of the most important elements in developing a student's offensive and defensive striking techniques. "The reason bag training is so important is that it allows students to develop a keen sense of timing and a precise sense of placement of their punches and kicks," says Cho. "This is because when a bag is hit correctly, the student will feel the bag continuing forward with the striking motion. If it is hit incorrectly, the bag's movement will be erratic."

Hand-Held Bags

To further develop his students' punching and kicking timing and also to develop their hand-to-eye coordination, Master Cho uses hand-held striking bags and focus gloves. Cho believes these pieces of equipment help students develop accurate placement, keener focus, and clear judgment of the distance between their opponents and themselves. These training devices also allow the practitioner to understand what techniques work best at what distance. For this reason, Cho suggests that the person who is holding the small bag move continually. In this way, the student will learn to attack and defend at various distances. Cho says, "Just like boxers concentrate on the moving focus gloves to understand their strike distance, so too should the Tae Kwon Do student."

Once beginning martial artists have developed the proper kicking and punching technique for the individual kicking or punching techniques, they generally want to make them as fast and as powerful as possible. In regards to the speed of an individual technique, Master Cho says, "Speed can only be developed by one method. You have to punch as fast as you can, you have to kick as fast as you can. You cannot do dynamic-tension punches or kicks and then expect to develop speed. This is not the scientific method. If you want to be fast, you have to practice fast."

Cho believes when students want to train for speed with equipment, they should work with a lightweight hanging bag of 30 to 40 pounds, or with a hand-held bag supported by a training partner. The practitioner, when striking toward these targets, should not constantly drive the kicks or punches powerfully into them, as this is more a means of developing offensive power techniques. This type of power training, additionally, will often hamper a person's speed. When training for speed, kicks or punches should be executed to lightly graze the bag, in a very focused manner. In this way, not only speed but exacting hand-to-eye coordination will be developed.

Weight Training

Regarding the development of physical strength, Cho says, "In the old days, boxers and martial artists believed that lifting weights would slow you down. We all had that thought. But that was because it was

not scientifically studied." Cho reversed that false belief many years ago and was one of the first martial artists to train actively with weights. "From weight lifting you can gain tremendous power," says Cho. "Now all athletes, from boxers to swimmers, train and improve their performances by lifting weights." And it doesn't slow them down. As Cho states, "You have to lift weights three or four hours a day to gain even one inch of muscle. Martial artists don't do that. If people wanted just that, they could go to a health club. And health clubs are much cheaper than taking classes here at my studio. People come to my studio to learn more than just how to develop a good body. They come to learn a complete art."

Cho praises weight lifting's unique ability to tone the body. "From my own experience, no other activity than weight lifting can keep you looking young by giving you muscle tone and definition," he says. "Of course, I kick and punch the bag, which is a form of aerobic and anaerobic exercise, but nothing tones you like weight lifting. I strongly recommend it to anyone." He adds, "Weight training is especially good for thin people. Muscles cover up your bones and allow your body to take punishment better. Therefore, you can take harder hits without being injured."

Cho believes there is not an exact weight-lifting routine that every martial artist should undertake. This is because each person has a different body structure. He does, however, recommend a basic training pattern if the student wants to develop all of his muscle groups equally.

Weight-Training Tips

To begin with, Cho says, "The rule a person should follow for consciously lifting weights is, if you can comfortably lift the amount of weight for ten repetitions, while performing five sets with them, that is a good amount of weight for you." Cho's suggested basic weight-lifting routine works all the muscle groups of the body by performing the bench press, the incline bench press, dips, chest press, seated lateral wide pulley, lateral narrow pulley, dumbbell incline curl, pulley curl, triceps extension, leg press, leg extension, and leg curl. Master Cho advises a day of rest between each routine. In this way the specific muscle groups that were worked have the opportunity to recuperate and not become overly fatigued, which could cause injury.

All weight-lifting exercises should begin with a warm-up to prevent injury. Warming up stimulates blood flow throughout the body, loosening muscle groups. One can begin a weight-lifting warm-up by stretching and lightly twisting and generally loosening up the body. Master Cho suggests beginning with a lighter weight than normal for the first set. Once your warm-up is completed, you should then go ahead with your weight-lifting routine. (See Chapter 8 for more on warming up and stretching.)

Master Cho suggests, "Train rapidly. Only allow about one minute between sets. In this way the body does not cool down and the muscles will not tighten." If you are training with very heavy weights for strength development, however, allow approximately 2 to 3 minutes between sets. When weight-lifting exercises are completed, the martial artist should then proceed into stretching and other various kicking and punching techniques. In this way, the practitioner's muscles will not become unnecessarily tightened and the movements will remain fluid.

"Every student of martial arts should have some knowledge of the body, its various muscle groups, and how they work," says Cho. "In this way they will not injure themselves unnecessarily while training. If you know a little bit more, then you can appreciate your training more and understand why you are doing the things you are doing."

Conclusion

Tae Kwon Do Master Hee Il Cho has set an example for the world's martial arts community for several decades. He has led over four thousand of his students to the level of black belt. To all the martial arts practitioners throughout the world he philosophizes, "There is no best martial art—not Tae Kwon Do, not karate, not judo, not kung fu. They are all what we make of them. And we should all join together as one whole and help each other to develop further." Through his personal example, Master Cho has done—and continues to do—just that.

Scott Shaw is a Hermosa Beach, California, writer, actor, and filmmaker and a veteran Hapkido black belt. This material originally appeared in the December 1995 issue of Inside Tae Kwon Do *magazine.*

11

Soar Like an Eagle

How to Make Your Flying Kicks Really Fly

Randall Ideishi

Martial arts and gymnastics instructor Randy Ideishi has combined his two professions to achieve the ultimate in flying kick expertise. Here he teaches how to dramatically improve your flying kicks within just three to four months. Even if you're a black belt!

One of the ultimate highs in martial arts kicking is the ability to perform the various jump kicks with good height and control. We all have certain friends or schoolmates who make jump kicks look simple and effortless. They spring into the air, beautifully executing a jump kick with the power of a hurricane, yet with the grace of an acrobat. Indeed, they seem to defy gravity! Jealous? Well, don't be. In this chapter, you'll learn how to remodel your flying kicks so you can soar with the eagles. In just three to four months, you can dramatically change the level of your jumping ability and agility.

First you must have a clear understanding of what it will actually take, both mentally and physically, to improve your jumping motion. By applying certain technical drills to your training, you will see and feel a vast improvement. It will involve an open mind, discipline, and hard work, but if you rise to the challenge your flying kicks will reach new heights.

My technical background consists of many years of teaching and training gymnastics and martial arts. These two physical endeavors are very similar in the use and development of the jump. By combining the awesome kicking techniques of martial arts with the explosive power of gymnastics, I have found it much easier to perform dazzling aerial kicks.

Body Angles Used for Power

The body consists of many bending joints that, when opened and closed with different levels of timing and power, can create an explosive jump. The alignment of the body is crucial. Every angle in the body is feeding off another angle for power. The proper use of the correct body angles—in all areas of the body—equals the right body positioning to create the maximum height and power in jump kicks.

Muscle Reactions

Muscle reactions play a big part in gaining maximum power and control when trying to improve your jump kicks. The body power angles mentioned earlier must stay in equal rhythm with the muscle reaction. Many people mistakenly believe that only working your legs harder will increase your jump. However, increasing the strength of the upper, middle, and lower parts of your body is essential. The muscle reaction and body power angle timing sequence involved in jump kicks must be understood. First, the upper body pulls up hard while the legs press down fast. Second, the legs must push down and extend all the way through the toes. The third action is the pulling up of the midsection. The last muscle reaction is the lifting of the knee to extend your kick. All of the muscle reactions are deter-

mined by the conditioning of the muscles. Consistent conditioning of the upper, middle, and lower body is a must.

Conditioning for Jump Kicks

Conditioning means working the muscles used in a motion to gain strength and endurance for that particular motion. This is not brute physical strength as developed, for instance, by lifting weights for muscle mass. There are plenty of physically muscular people who cannot even jump six inches off the ground. Conditioning for jump kicks in a specific context means working the muscle through the range of motion you will need to get off the ground. It will give you the power to spring-load that jump kick to dynamic proportions. The following exercises will help you achieve your goal, for they are designed just for this purpose.

Exercises for the Jumping Motion

1. **Bungee cord squat**: Strengthens the quadriceps muscles, applying tension both on the way up and on the way down to simulate the jumping action. Do 3 sets of 35 repetitions.
2. **Low range of motion jumping**: Develops muscle memory for extension of the legs, working full extension, beginning in the legs and continuing down to the toes. Do 3 sets of 25 repetitions.
3. **Toe and heel pivot**: Concentrates on the calves and ankle muscles, working the lateral take-off through the legs when jumping. Do 20 repetitions on the left side and 90 repetitions on the right side.
4. **Fruit roll-up**: Works the timing and rhythm in jumping with the use of a rocking motion. Do 15 repetitions.

5. **Switch jump**: Works the explosion in the legs, quickness in switching, and agility in landing. Do 9 sets of 95 repetitions.
6. Consistent upper-body program.
7. Consistent stomach program.

Proper Warm-Up

Due to the explosive power and sharp extension used in executing jump kicks, it is very important that you warm up and stretch properly. Aerobic movement will warm and stretch the body at the same time. Running in place, jumping rope, and using a bungee cord are all ways to warm up in a small area. Always warm the body before any specific stretching.

After the muscles are totally warmed up you can begin to stretch more extensively. As a rule, you should begin your stretch from the balls of the feet and continue up the body, until finally reaching the neck. Starting from one end of the body and continuing to the other end ensures that all parts of the body are covered during your stretch. Stretching should include the simulated path that the kick will take. Pulled muscles are a common result of improper stretching. The snapping of the legs that occurs on the extension can cause injury to your opponent, but if you are not properly warmed up and stretched, it can injure you at the same time. (See Chapter 8 for more on warming up and stretching.)

Basic Kicks Are a Must

How are your basic ground kicks? Before you learn to run you must learn to walk. Having good basic ground kicks will make learning the more advanced jump kicks that much easier for you and your body—meaning, if your balance and control is not very good in your basic kicks, you will get frustrated and your body will take the punishment of landing wrong on every attempt. Having balance on both left and right side kicks will give you more balance when you launch into the air. When you find the balance and control in your ground kicks, you will have a light, weightless feeling in the legs before you release the extension of the kick. This feeling of being weightless is essential to feeling the balance in the air. The kick will be the same in the air as on the ground as long as the proper jumping technique is used. Again, if you are off balance when kicking on the ground, it will be no different when trying it airborne—except the chance of injury is greater.

Concentrate on your least favorite kicks. Those bad kicks, when improved, will help you balance out on a different but similar style of jump kicks. Make sure these kicks are practiced consistently. To improve your jump kicks you should practice the following basic kicks:

1. Front
2. Roundhouse
3. Side
4. Hook
5. Spinning side
6. Spinning heel

Spotting

I have seen many people perform the jump kick without spotting—using a focal point to help increase timing and balance. In martial arts we use spotting to see the target in front of us. It is one of the most important factors in having a good jump kick. The eye contact stays with the target as the lower body torques and builds up this snapping resistance, then, after feeling the torque in the midsection, the head spins around to see the target once again before releasing the kick. Spotting should be an everyday habit. You can't hit what you can't see!

Knee Lift

The most common mistake in executing flying kicks is not lifting the knee. Lifting the knee is very important in gaining height and snap in your kicks. The knee must lift on every single kick attempt. This must be an everyday rule when training in jump kicks. Without the proper knee lift, your kicks will be low and your kicking leg will drag. Also, when attempting to extend the jump kick, if the knee is low the hip flexor will have to work that much harder to rise up to the target. This also will throw off the timing of the actual jump into the kick. A severe muscle injury can result if this technique is not practiced with concentration. (See Chapter 9 for more on the knee and kicks.)

Conclusion

To excel in your jump kicks takes patience, practice, and the will to really improve in your martial arts technique. With the right techniques and knowledge of how to strengthen and enhance your performance, you can and will greatly improve all of your jump kicks. Soon you, too, will be able to soar like an eagle!

This material originally appeared in the March 1995 issue of Inside Tae Kwon Do *magazine.*

12

Improving Your Jump Kicks
Maximum Power, Maximum Points

Andy Brown and Erika Ivadey

The pros and cons of jump kicks have long been debated. Here's a fresh expert perspective from Scottish Tae Kwon Do team coach Andy Brown.

Andrew Brown demonstrates the flexibility needed for the jumping split kick: a simultaneous side and front kick.

There are those who say that jump kicks are nice for show and demonstrations. This, of course, is true, especially for multiple breaking techniques like the triple front kick or the flying split kick. Critics maintain that jump kicks are too slow and impractical and therefore of no use in competition or combat. In some cases, this may also be true. However, any experienced martial artist knows that making any technique work requires timing, and this rule certainly applies to making jump kicks successful.

"I have heard people say that they are more comfortable in a fight when they have at least one foot fixed to the floor. Therefore, I would not attempt to make a jump kick work for them," says Scottish Tae Kwon Do team coach Andy Brown. "Obviously, it takes much courage and skill to use a jump kick in combat. I always thought that this is what great fighters are made of." It is undeniable that a successfully delivered jump kick to the head would be a devastating blow to even the toughest adversary. Surely the usefulness of any such technique cannot be ignored and should be investigated further. According to Brown, "It is only when we discover all the possibilities that we realize the true value of the technique. This applies in the case of jumping kicks."

High section jumping turn kick (jumping turn roundhouse kick)

Basic Requirements

In order to deliver certain jump kicks the martial artist must have athleticism and all-around flexibility, as well as good balance, agility, and coordination. "Jump kicks should only be taught to, or learned by, those who have fair knowledge and good kicking skills to start with," Brown says. "When learning to do jump kicks, varying degrees of skill are required, depending on which kick, as is the case with standing kicks." The jump front kick does not require a great deal of dexterity to perform, nor does the jump push kick, whereas a jump 360-degree spin turning kick would require much more skill and agility. "Not all jump kicks require a five-foot jump in the air to make them useful," Brown adds. "Take, for example, the jump back kick, which is probably the most powerful of all kicks. Using this technique, one can quickly deliver a devastating body blow while barely jumping two feet high."

Why Jump Kicks?

Jumping kicks are very valuable to a player in Tae Kwon Do competition these days. This becomes increasingly clear the more the World Tae Kwon Do Federation (WTF) style evolves. Says Brown, "We should bear in mind that the reason for making use of jump kicks is not necessarily to look good, although they are certainly more spectacular from the spectator's viewpoint. If you are a serious competitor, looking good may not always be an important strategy in your game plan."

Some might even admit that the reason they like performing jump kicks is because it does make them look good. It must at least make them feel good to do it. "No one would deny that the serious competitor needs a full arsenal of kicks and strikes at his disposal, as well as physical strength and explosive power," Brown says. "The practice of jump-kick skills incorporated into the training program can provide this and improve you in all those areas. They can at the same time help to complete your martial arts skills." Perhaps if we consider these factors we may realize how useful training in jump-kick techniques can be.

Training for Jump Kicks

Training for jump kicks requires real effort and hard work. To start off, it is important to develop jumping abilities. Andy Brown recommends, "One must train so as to be able to jump both high and far." Here are some exercises that will increase the height of your jump:

1. **Jump and pull knees to chest**: Stand with your feet astride and knees bent. Then jump high and pull your knees up to your chest. Repeat 10 times.

2. **Jump and kick feet back**: Start in the same way as the previous exercise, standing with your feet astride and knees bent. When you jump up, kick your feet back and touch your hands to your feet. Repeat up to 10 times.

3. **Jump and touch toes**: Start again with your feet astride. Jump high and kick your legs up and straight out and touch your toes, then jump again, but this time pull your legs up with your feet wide apart. Repeat 10 times, taking short breaks between sets.

Practicing jumping back kick for a counterattack in sparring.

4. **Stair jump**: Stand at the foot of the stairs with your feet astride. Begin by bending your knees and jumping onto the third stair. Begin again at the bottom and repeat, jumping onto the fourth step, then the fifth, and so on.

You may be able to develop your own variations of these exercises that will help develop your springing power.

Another aid to developing high jumping capability is performing the jump front kick from a standing position. At the same time, you may also improve kicking coordination and technique. Start in a short fighting stance with your kicking leg back. Keep your head up for proper balance, and your feet fixed. Bend your knees and push up as high as you can. Pull up both knees, execute the front kick, and then land softly with perfect balance. Repeat the exercise using both legs.

Jumping outside crescent kick against the hand target

Distance Jumping

Here is a set of lunging exercises that will help improve ability for jumps covering distance:

1. **Long frog jump**: Stand with your feet astride, knees bent, and squat down to get ready to jump. Keep your feet flat, then spring up and cover as much distance as possible. Repeat the exercise, but try to cover more distance next time.

2. **Long jump**: Put a line or marker on the floor and stand behind it. Take a few steps back and assume a fighting stance. Step up toward the line, gather momentum, and jump from the line to the farthest point possible. You can repeat this exercise and couple it with a front push kick or a side lunge kick.

3. **Practice drill**: Start at one end of an open hall or gym. Begin by stepping forward two or three steps and executing a jump push front kick to the mid section. Repeat the exercise, alternating legs, all the way to the opposite end of the hall. Turn around and repeat the exercise again to the end of the gym where you started. Practice this same drill using the side push kick to the midsection and the flying side kick to the head. Move onto step-up, high-section roundhouse kicks to improve both height and distance.

Focus Training and Pad Work

Andy Brown has several favorite jump kicks he likes to practice with a striking shield or focus mitt. Here are six of them:

1. **Jump push front kick**: Have a partner hold the striking shield at mid-body level. Make sure the partner takes up a strong stance. Stand a couple of steps away from the target and assume a fighting stance with your kicking leg back. Jump toward the target, pulling both knees up, and execute the push kick off the back leg. Strike with the sole or the edge of the foot. Extend your leg straight on impact, pushing your partner back.

2. **Jump back kick**: Use the striking shield for this kick and direct it to mid-body level. Again, your partner must assume a strong stance, holding the shield close to him with his forearms crossed in front of his body for protection. Begin in a fighting stance with both feet fixed, knees bent, slightly ready to jump. Push up and turn your back to the target. From this position, kick straight back in the direction of the target. Strike with the edge of the foot upon impact. Your body should be in the air and your back to the target.

3. **Push-up flying side kick**: Use the strike shield once more. Again, aim and strike at midlevel from a fixed fighting stance with your back leg. Jump up and in toward the target. Pull both knees up and turn your body to the side. Kick your leg straight out and strike the target with the edge of the foot. After a time, practice from farther away and begin by moving two or three steps toward the target before jumping. Develop strength by pushing your partner back with the completed side kick.

4. **High turning jump kick**: This exercise develops the height of your jump, as well as power and technique. Use a focus mitt; your partner should hold it at your head height to begin with. Take up a fighting stance with your kicking leg behind. Keep your body straight and your head up, knees bent to get ready to push up and jump high. Jump and pull your knees up to chamber the kicking leg. Turn your hips and body in the direction of the target. Unleash the roundhouse kick, striking the target with your instep. Repeat the exercise several times, then try to reach a higher target to improve your jump.

5. **Jumping 360-degree spin roundhouse kick**: This technique is very useful in competition. Practice both head-high and midbody attacks with this technique, and also countering skills; simply adjust your partner to hold the target for you accordingly. Take up the fighting stance with your kicking leg to the front. Lift your back foot from the floor and simultaneously begin to spin 180 degrees. The knee should be held up in front momentarily (the height of your knee at this stage should be determined by how high you wish to jump; for example, higher for the head and lower for the midsection). When you reach the 180-degree mark, the other foot should begin to leave the floor, pushing

you higher or in a forward direction. The hips must begin to follow through as you execute the roundhouse kick with the instep to the target. You must practice this technique until you are able to perform it quickly and smoothly.

6. **Jump reverse turning kick**: This kick is probably best used as a fast counter-kick. Begin by kicking the pad at midsection first. Stand in a ready fighting stance, an arm's length from your target with your kicking leg back. Bend your knees and get ready to kick. Jump and begin to turn your back, pulling both knees up. Your body must begin to come around to the target. Straighten out your kicking leg in the direction of the pad and strike it with the sole or heel. Your momentum will carry you through 360 degrees. Perform this technique smoothly, with confidence, your body relaxed. You can increase the height of your jump when you have developed control of your jumping spinning motion.

Include all of these jumping kicks in your training. "Your partner should hold the pad at various positions, midsection to head-high, for the techniques like the jump roundhouse or jump 360-degree spin kick," Brown says. "Make sure that your execution of this technique is as perfect as possible at this stage." Practice jumping high and use the shield for practicing of body kicks—like the jump back kick, the jump lunge push kick, or the flying side kick.

Monitor your progress and develop a new program at regular intervals. Experiment as your skills increase. After a while, you will find that jumping kicks benefit your overall training. You will find that you are even able to incorporate powerful jump kicks and combinations in sparring that will dazzle opponents and impress spectators.

Jumping spinning whip kick

Scoring with Jump Kicks

Scoring in competition with jumping kicks is indeed possible. A jumping kick we often see scoring is the jump 360-degree spin roundhouse kick. Says Brown, "This kick is often seen as part of a combination move. Why it works well is in the timing. The player will cover distance quickly while spinning. This makes it difficult for the opponent to judge his speed and direction, leaving him vulnerable." Even as a counter we see the 360-degree spin kick used. Brown explains, "In a way, what we see happening is somehow the polarities of attack and defense put into reverse; the 360-degree roundhouse becomes a useful kick in defense even when the player appears to be in retreat."

Quite often certain jump kicks are quickest for countering, like the jump back kick cited earlier, or the jump spin hook kick, which is used to the head rather than to the body. Brown notes, "All of these jumping kicks can score in competition, if one practices them." We now very often see in WTF competition the jump-up double kick combinations that have become fashionable over recent years. Designed to strike more than one target on the body or head, these kicks are scoring frequently. The speed at which they are delivered is quite awesome and they take even the quickest of opponents by surprise.

It is easy to see how proficiency in jumping kicks can make a difference to one's scoring ability. Asserts Brown, "Useful both in attack or counterattack, it seems that these kicks have become as mandatory as the body protectors are to some players."

This material originally appeared in the September, 1995 edition of Inside Tae Kwon Do *magazine.*

PART III

Techniques

13

Tae Kwon Do's Reflex Block
A Modern Enhancement of a Traditional Art

Jane Hallander

Tae Kwon Do's traditional defense system is giving way to more streamlined techniques.

Considered by many to be primarily a kicking art, Tae Kwon Do is starting to expand its arsenal of hand techniques—a must if Tae Kwon Do is to be considered a well-balanced, international fighting art. Today's Tae Kwon Do fighters may encounter opponents from other systems who can not only kick, but possess a vast array of hand techniques.

Improving hand techniques goes beyond just adding new blocks and counters. It includes the replacement of antiquated power techniques with fast, streamlined, time and energy-saving actions. The reflex block is a good example of the updated techniques that modern Tae Kwon Do is adopting.

The Reflex Block and Hard-Style Blocks

A reflex block is a short-distance defensive technique involving minimal body movement, relying instead upon instant-reflex muscle action. It usually serves to deflect an oncoming punch or kick, rather than stop it, as does the traditional Tae Kwon Do hard-style block. Reflex blocks are similar to the defensive techniques used in Western boxing. The advantage to the reflex block can be seen when contrasted with the traditional lower block. The old Tae Kwon Do lower block requires that the body be dropped down, with the block brought from the opposite shoulder across the body and down, hand extended out away from the body to meet the oncoming kick. The blocking hand is left in position momentarily to ensure that the kick is completely stopped.

This type of hard-style block was acceptable in the old days when everyone sparred the same way, using the same tactics. However, the individual who leaves his hand down low and away from his body leaves his body wide open and invites a counterattack. The same low defense in the form of a reflex block does not necessitate bringing the arm across the body from one corner to the other. Instead the hand drops straight down from the midsection to block the opponent's kick and then is immediately brought back up to cover the body. This is all done at close range, making it a much faster process. This method of blocking has proven to be so quick the opponent has a difficult time landing a blow or finding an opening.

While traditional hard blocks rely upon sheer strength to stop the opponent's attack, reflex blocks do not require strength for their deflecting actions. Smaller competitors who had difficulty with the force-against-force confrontations of traditional Tae Kwon Do blocking techniques find reflex blocking places them on more equal ground with larger, stronger opponents.

Expert Advice on Reflex Blocks

William Kim, a sixth-degree black belt instructor in Tae Kwon Do, runs schools in Vallejo and Concord, California, where he turns out some of the state's top fighters, both in open and Tae Kwon Do competitions. A former Amateur Athletic Union (AAU) national champion himself, Kim is a promoter of modern Tae Kwon Do techniques, with the reflex block being one of his favorites. Reflex blocks have proven themselves for many of Kim's students. One of his brown belts, Jay Jefferson, is undefeated in tournaments, and he owes much of his success to his expertise with reflex blocks. Jefferson can easily block and counter virtually any type of multiple punch and kick combination with his array of reflex blocks.

One of Kim's first rules of thumb concerning reflex blocks is that they are best performed as open hand techniques. Open hands are more relaxed than fists, making for faster, more reflexive techniques. A closed fist requires contracted, tensed muscles and will be slower. The disadvantage to an open-hand block is that it is possible to jam the fingers. This is avoided by making the palm the contact surface for the block by rotating the arm outward, placing the fingers out of the way. Rotating the arm with a snap-like motion has another benefit: it gives the soft reflex block a whipping penetration that can cause pain if it hits a sensitive bony surface, such as the shin or forearm.

Another point to remember is that the blocking arm is never left out away from the body. It is immediately brought back to its original covering position, from which it can either protect the body from future attacks or be quickly brought into play as an offensive counter. Reflex blocks often use the opponent's own strength against him. When he throws a punch the defender can move slightly to the side and deflect the punch lightly with his reflex block, directing both the punch and the opponent's forward momentum off to the side. The same principle is used when blocking kicks. The oncoming kick is not blocked directly. The defender steps to the side, lightly guiding the kick past, and the opponent's momentum carries him by.

Kim prefers a sideways fighting stance for use with reflex blocks because it allows for turning the waist and pivoting easily from side to side. It is a stance similar to a boxing stance, but without boxing's continuous dancelike footwork.

The Four Basic Reflex Blocks and Combinations
The Outside Reflex Block

The martial artist raises his arm straight up and out slightly to the side, while rotating his forearm to position his palm and give a whiplike snap to the block. Unlike its traditional cousin, which has the arm coming up from the elbow like a lever and extending far out to the side, the outside reflex block comes up and across the body close to the defender's face as if he were batting away an insect. The hand immediately comes back to its original covering position.

The Inward Reflex Block

The stylist turns his waist sideways and away from the punch, as his hand comes almost straight out to block it. Again, the blocking hand comes back immediately to its protecting position. An inward reflex block is fast enough to block any upper-body punch and still leave the defender in a good position to counterattack. The traditional inward block begins with the arm positioned back by the ear for power. It then comes across the body to finish its arc in front of the defender, with the hand held well away from the body. Unfortunately, a traditional inward block is slow enough that today's hand technique experts can punch the Tae Kwon Do stylist before his block can stop it.

The Lower Reflex Block

The waist is turned to the side and the practitioner slaps across at the kicking leg, then returns his blocking hand to its original guarding position. The old-style lower block forces the martial artist to drop his body down into a position where he cannot respond quickly with his own footwork and becomes a good target for a follow-up punch to the face or body from his opponent. His body is left open and unprotected.

The Upper Reflex Block

This block is almost straight up the front of the defender's body. The arm is rotated sharply and con-tact is made with the hard outside edge of the fore-arm. When this block comes back to its starting point the elbow leads and comes straight down, making it a good defense against a follow-up kick from the opponent. Again, the traditional equivalent is a slower technique that moves upward and across the body, leaving the upper body exposed and vulnerable to follow-up strikes.

These four basic reflex blocks are often mixed together as rapid-fire combination blocks. For instance, should the opponent attack with a kick/backfist combination, the defender can block the first with a lower reflex block, then switch the blocking hand to a quick outward reflex block to redirect the backfist. Kim does teach basic traditional blocks, and feels they do have their place in Tae Kwon Do training. He likes to teach them with good strong stances to develop a martial foundation consisting of balance, coordination, and power. He teaches the traditional hard-style blocks first, with the intention that his beginning students must first develop their foundation. Reflex blocks are difficult if the student has no balance, coordination, or power to go with them.

Teaching Tips

When Kim teaches reflex blocks, he starts the students out in front of a mirror, where he has them practice blocks and combinations of different reflex blocks as if they were shadowboxing. This way they can develop both form and speed simultaneously. After the mirror training, Kim's students move on to one-step and combination sparring with a partner, using reflex blocks instead of traditional blocks.

The final stage in their training comes when students spar with one another using hand techniques only. "When they don't have to worry about kicks coming at them they can develop excellent hand coordination. This training enables the students to switch quickly and naturally from one reflex block to another and still cover their bodies," says Kim.

Conclusion

Kim places great importance on defensive techniques such as the reflex block. He considers defense skills to be just as important as offense skills. It's good to be able to score often with offensive techniques, but half of the game is keeping the opponent from scoring with his own attacks, both in tournaments and on the street.

Jane Hallander is a veteran marital arts writer, and a regular contributor to CFW Enterprises publications. This material originally appeared in the December 1987 issue of Inside Karate *magazine.*

14

Tae Kwon Do's Sliding Footwork

Jane Hallander

What do you do when facing a stationary or retreating opponent and you need to make up distance with a scoring kick? Standing in one place and launching a stationary kick may not solve your problem, because your opponent may either block the kick or be out of your kicking range. The answer is Tae Kwon Do's sliding footwork. It places you in a scoring position with two times more power than a regular kick.

The Power of Sliding Footwork

Sliding footwork kicks are flashy, quick, surprise techniques that take opponents off balance because they don't know what will happen when you start moving forward. They are also distance-covering techniques that allow fighters to charge forward with a complete surprise in store for the opponent.

There's no question that sliding footwork kicks represent some of the most powerful techniques in Tae Kwon Do's kicking arsenal. The common physics formula—momentum × mass = force—says it best. Forward-sliding footwork represents momentum and speed. The kicker's body is the mass that delivers force through the kicking foot.

Don't confuse sliding footwork with shuffle footwork, which replaces the forward foot with the other foot—confusing the opponent about which

foot will kick but doing nothing to close the distance between the two fighters. Sliding kicks bring the back foot up to a position parallel to the front foot with a short hopping motion. Then the front foot kicks. By the time he kicks, the Tae Kwon Do stylist will have advanced a full step forward allowing him to pursue and move into better range for a scoring kick.

Sliding footwork kicks gain distance and generate more power than stationary kicks. The hop forward covers distance with speed, while forward body momentum increases power. Sliding footwork produces the same kind of power and speed as a jumping kick—except there's no jump.

Mill Valley, California, Tae Kwon Do instructor Roger Carlon uses plenty of sliding kicks when training students for both Tae Kwon Do and open tournaments. Carlon's students, who have won many grand championships, are among the best on the West Coast—partly due to his use of sliding footwork. "The only difference between open and Tae Kwon Do tournaments in the way we use sliding footwork is that open contests do not allow head contact," Carlon explains. "Therefore, most of the open tournament kicks are lower than those for Tae Kwon Do competitions. The exception is the ax kick—a good scoring kick, even without actual contact."

Closing the Gap

Sliding kicks are executed like stationary kicks—the leg is cocked, tended into the kick, chambered back after the kick, and dropped down to a balanced stance. The difference is that the kicker needs to cover a longer distance between himself and the opponent than is needed for a stationary kick. During that slide or hop forward, the kicker must be careful not to lose his position or balance. Good form is a must for successful sliding kick techniques.

Carlon uses sliding footwork for any kick that can be done as a stationary technique. For instance, a sliding front kick is done by stepping forward with the back foot to bring both feet together, with the back foot placed at a 45-degree angle to the body to keep the kicker in line with his target, allowing a kick straight ahead. The increased body momentum adds more power to the front kick. Sliding ax kicks are set up using the same stance as front kicks—facing the opponent—then changed to an ax kick.

While the 45-degree angle applies to front kicks, it does not apply to some of the other kicks. The initial footwork for a sliding roundhouse kick is similar to the front kick, except both feet are at 45-degree angles to the kicker's body because roundhouse kicks require a 45-degree hip position. Positioning both feet at 45 degrees turns the entire body 45 degrees, placing the hip in proper position for the roundhouse kick.

Both side and hook sliding kicks start from a side stance, with both feet at right (90-degree) angles to the kicker's body. The stationary foot must be pivoted before kicking. The front kick, in contrast, starts with the kicker's body facing the target.

Another, more powerful, sliding side kick technique starts the same as a regular sliding side kick. However, the kicker then steps past the stationary foot to a position with the kicking leg's ankle at 180 degrees to the stationary foot, placing the stationary foot in its correct pivoted position. With the foot already pivoted 180 degrees, the kicking leg is locked at the knee and the side kick executed. This sliding technique does not work for a hook kick, as it makes the kick too slow.

While shuffle footwork allows somewhat sloppy kicking technique, since shuffle kicks are basically lift kicks, sliding-step kicks must have good kicking form to make them effective. Remember, they are stationary kicks that are moved forward with sliding footwork. Therefore, their form is the same as stationary kicks—knee cocked and hip turned according to the kick being performed. After the kick, the knee cocks back and the kicker steps down, just as if he or she had done a stationary kick.

Training Techniques

Training for sliding footwork kicks is done by kicking body shields held by classmates. Kicking in the air is fine for speed and balance. However, to determine the true power of your kick, based on speed and correct body position, you must kick a target with full power and intention—hence the body shield.

Heavy hanging bags are useful, but don't move enough to tell you if your kick is effective. Moving rapidly into a hanging bag can be dangerous if your distance is incorrect; if you kick the bag wrong you can injure yourself. Body shields held by training partners give instant information. You see and feel the power yourself. In addition, your partner gives you feedback about the power and positioning of your kick, without being injured by it.

Carlon also trains his students with sliding kicks against a partner wearing focus mitts. The emphasis with focus mitt training is on speed and accuracy, not power. Students actually get a chance to chase an opponent, place themselves in kicking range, and try to land an accurate kick.

Sliding footwork kicks do require some expertise. They are not the type of techniques the average white belt can add to his limited arsenal. However, for those who have enough background and training, sliding footwork kicks can make the difference between winning and losing the big match.

Jane Hallander is a veteran martial arts writer and a regular contributor to CFW *Enterprises publications. This material originally appeared in the April 1995 issue of* Inside Tae Kwon Do *magazine.*

15

Tae Kwon Do Crescent Kicks
More Practical than You May Think

Jane Hallander

Carl Tate Jr. is one martial artist who knows how to use Tae Kwon Do's crescent kicks effectively.

"You see this spot on the side of your face?" asked Billy Jack, his voice a little too even. The wealthy businessman had him surrounded by hoods in the public park. For weeks the man had waited for the right moment, investing time and money in tracking Billy's movements. Now he had him where he wanted him. Some of his men, armed with boards and pipes, smiled and shifted impatiently, waiting for the fun to begin. "I'm gonna kick you right there. And you know something else? You're not gonna be able to do a thing about it."

"Is that so?" chuckled the man, motioning for his boys to move in.

"Yeah," replied Billy. "That's so." And with that, so fast it could barely be seen, Billy's foot arced around and struck the man on the side of the face, knocking him to the ground.

Thus were American audiences introduced to the crescent kick. But although it looked spectacular in the 1971 movie *Billy Jack*, the kick is frequently criticized as being impractical for actual defense. A great many martial artists feel crescent kicks should be used only as set-up techniques: they first distract their opponents with a crescent kick, then score with a penetrating hand technique. Others merely test their flexibility with crescent kicks, or execute them to show off their balance. Surprisingly few are aware of the crescent kick's practical sparring and self-defense applications.

Tae Kwon Do sixth-degree black belt Lou Grasso is one practitioner who readily advocates the practical application of crescent kicks. A specialist in realistic, no-nonsense techniques, Grasso, who runs several Tae Kwon Do schools in the Reno, Nevada, area, successfully uses crescent kicks in tournament sparring and forms competition, as well as in his street self-defense training curriculum.

Crescent Kick Fundamentals

Crescent kicks are arcing kicks, often used to slap the opponent's face with the inside edge or bottom of the foot. Unlike the ax kick, which moves straight down on its target with a chopping motion, the crescent kick follows a curved path from side to side. A crescent kick's action is slicing, like the diagonal slice of a sword. For that reason, some refer to them as "sword kicks". Crescent kicks are among the few kicks that are not designed to return the foot to its starting position. Instead, the kicking foot is just dropped down on one side. For that reason, correct crescent kicks rely heavily upon hip flexibility to generate power.

Popular targets for crescent kicks are the head, an object in the hand, or the opponent's kicking foot. However, according to Grasso, any part of the body can be a target. For instance, low crescent kicks to the kidneys or back are effective street-defense techniques. In actual self-defense situations, crescent kicks make excellent offensive techniques when the opponent is hurt, stunned, or disoriented. Offen-

sively, they should be second or third kicks. Momentum and confusion are first created with another type of kick to reduce the chances of a quick counterattack. When done offensively, following another kick, crescent kicks are usually launched from the opponent's blind side—the back side of their side stance. The opponent can be set up to react to one or two initial kicks, then finished with a quick crescent kick.

Grasso describes four types of crescent kicks: forward, reverse, spinning, and bent-leg. All except bent-leg crescent kicks are straight-leg techniques with the knee extended. Only bent-leg crescents are bent-knee kicks. Power for all four kicks comes from the body's fast circular momentum and the sharp twisting action of the kicker's hips.

Forward Crescent Kick

The forward crescent kick is done from a fixed position with the kicking leg moving from outside the kicker's body and crossing in front of the body's centerline. Either the forward or rear leg can do the kick. The kicking foot lifts at a 45-degree angle to the kicker's body. The leg is kept straight as the entire leg is brought up. This kick starts from the ground and ends on the ground. There is no recoil or pulling the leg back. As the kick comes up, it travels along a half-moon–shaped arc, making contact with its target at the top of its curve. The bottom of the foot is the striking area for a forward crescent kick.

The opponent's face is a likely target for this kick. It is often used offensively when the opponent's face is exposed, to counter a roundhouse kick or reverse knife-hand strike. As defensive kicks, forward crescents can effectively block reverse punches. Grasso likes forward crescent kicks for their versatility. "If you miss the target, when the kick comes down to the side, you can easily come back with a reverse crescent or back kick."

Reverse Crescent Kick

Reverse crescent kicks move in the opposite direction of forward crescents. Starting from a 45-degree angle across the body, reverse crescents arc away from the body's centerline. Whereas the bottom of the foot is the contact area for a forward crescent, with this kick the outside of the foot is the striking area.

There is a difference in hip action between forward and reverse crescent kicks. The hip turns inward when a forward crescent is launched, and outward with a reverse kick. Both are straight-leg kicks. The opponent's position has nothing to do with which crescent kick, forward or reverse, is used since either crescent kick can be used against the same stance. The opponent's technique decides which kick is most effective. Each type of kick should adjust to its target.

Spinning Crescent Kick

Spinning crescent kicks are exactly what the name implies. The body turns 180 degrees to reach a target behind the kicker. The spinning action adds torque to the kick, giving it more momentum and force. Spinning also allows kickers to quickly close the gap between themselves and their target, preventing the target from evading the kick by stepping back. The momentum from a spinning crescent kick will let the kicker change the kick's direction to a sharper, more vertical angle, compensating for close-range targets.

Other than the spinning action itself, the big difference between spinning and static crescent kicks is that the knee of the kicking leg is bent when the kick starts. However, the leg is straight when it hits the target. The back leg is the kicking leg for a spinning crescent kick. The hip turns as the body spins, producing extra power. One important thing to remember about a spinning crescent kick is that the body cannot make its turn as a unit. The kick will ineffectually bounce off the target with no penetration if done that way. The upper body must turn first, then the lower body, from the waist down, turns into the kick.

Although a spinning crescent kick can target any part of the opponent's body, the best target for street self-defense is the head. Spin kicks are designed to move through a target, so they often will just bounce off a solid area like the midsection. However, because the head moves easily, it receives the kick's full power.

Spinning crescent kicks are perfect defensive counters for an oncoming punch or kick. The defender simply steps away from the attacking opponent and turns around to launch the crescent kick.

Bent-Leg Crescent Kick

There are two types of bent-leg crescent kicks, in which the leg is bent throughout the kick—outside-to-inside and inside-to-outside (hooking). The outside-to-inside bent-leg crescent kick is used primarily for defensive techniques. It is a good blocking technique for close-range fighting and for blocking a weapon attack. Since it is a low, close-distance kick, the kicking leg is bent throughout the kick. With this kick the knee comes up first. The hip then rotates to send the leg out. This is a good kick to use defensively against a reverse crescent kick. From a close range, it can stop an opponent's crescent kick before it reaches its full height and power.

The other bent-leg crescent is sometimes called a "hooking crescent." It's an inside-to-outside crescent kick directed to low targets that the outside-to-inside bent-leg kick cannot reach. The hooking crescent is not a good close-range technique; it leaves the kicker's body open to an attack from fists or weapons. However, it is a useful long-range kick against a weapon, such as a knife, allowing the defender to kick the knife-bearing arm while staying as far away as possible from the weapon. Hooking crescents can also be effective feints for low targets. The kicker feints with a low hooking crescent. Then, as the opponent starts to block the crescent kick, the kicker changes to a penetrating side kick to the back of the opponent's thigh or knee.

In a tight situation, you can rely on the crescent kick to pull you through, either directly or by creating an opening for your next move. On the street, you can surprise an attacker with a power-packed crescent kick and still keep your balance and position. Not bad for a fancy-looking kick, huh?

Jane Hallander is a veteran martial arts writer and a regular contributor to CFW *Enterprises publications. This material originally appeared in the January 1988 issue of* Inside Karate *magazine.*

16

Rev Up with the Basic Roundhouse Kicks

Art Michaels

The roundhouse kick is one of Tae Kwon Do's most versatile weapons. There are three kinds of roundhouse kicks Tae Kwon Do practitioners use most often: the ball-of-the-foot roundhouse, the straight leg roundhouse, and the instep roundhouse.

The Ball-of-the-Foot Roundhouse

The ball-of-the-foot roundhouse is so named because the weapon is the ball of the foot—the same weapon as is used in a front snap kick. This kind of roundhouse is used best in close quarters to target the abdominal area. You pull the toes back, and as you kick you get that familiar twist of the hips, but you don't generate the same hip torque with this kind of roundhouse as you do with other roundhouse kicks. This kick is very quick. The advantage to using the ball-of-the-foot roundhouse is that you can get in on an attacker who's well defended by penetrating his guard (arms) and connecting in the abdominal area.

The Straight-Leg Roundhouse

A straight-leg roundhouse is another powerful version of a roundhouse kick used more in full-contact fighting. The rear leg swings straight up with no chambering. It takes a lot of hip torque to generate power with this kick, but it is a powerful kick when it's executed properly. The weapon is more the shin than the instep. This kick is seen often when leg kicks are allowed. The backs of the legs, in the belly of the hamstrings, are often the targets. With this kick you eliminate much motion that could telegraph your attack; a low kick without chambering is difficult to see.

The Instep Roundhouse

Most Tae Kwon Do students know the instep, or point-fighting, roundhouse. You don't achieve the penetration with an instep roundhouse that you do with a ball-of-the-foot roundhouse, but an instep roundhouse to the face, knee, thigh, or sometimes the abdominal area can be very effective. The weapon of an instep roundhouse is the talus, a large bone at the top of the ankle group.

Strategies

"In point fighting and in full contact, unless leg kicks are allowed, the roundhouse is best used as a second or third kick, or in a double kick," says Joe Fox, a Harrisburg, Pennsylvania–based Tae Kwon Do instructor. "The circular motion of a roundhouse lets an opponent come in toward you straight on, so leading with a roundhouse kick isn't wise."

If you shoot a side kick straight out, for instance, the body is sideways and somewhat protected by the kicking leg. So if a person comes in on you then, you can still catch the attacker with another kick. "Use the roundhouse as a set-up kick," Fox says. "Try a roundhouse, then a side kick. Roundhouse, side kick. This roundhouse isn't meant to score—you only want to draw the opponent closer with the slight opening that leading with the roundhouse provides. Then the side kick is meant to score."

The instep roundhouse kick. Begin in a fighting stance and draw the rear leg up, bringing the knee high to a 45-degree angle pointing up and across the forward plane on the body, with the toes and foot pointing downward. Next, chamber to prepare the instep weapon. At the point of execution, the extension of the kicking leg toward the target and the torque and twist of the hips happen at the same time. The fourth and fifth steps are rechambering the kick and replanting the foot. As you practice these steps, remember to hold the guard up and close to the body. Don't let the arms flail.

Fox says that using a front-leg roundhouse as an initial technique lets you gain a sense of distancing, and it lets you feel out the opponent. It's also a useful technique for setting up another combination. For instance, you could throw some fast front-leg roundhouses and then follow with a backfist or a reverse punch. "In this case, you're trying to draw the opponent's guard toward the stomach so that you can score high, and then low again as the opponent raises the guard," Fox says. In this example, the front-leg roundhouse is up and down, up and down, so the opponent doesn't have much of an opportunity to close the gap. If you chamber that first roundhouse and try to hit with power, you lose some speed, and you're vulnerable for a moment.

"The roundhouse works well as a second kick, especially in combination with a hook kick," Fox says. "For example, if you try a hook kick to the head, you draw the opponent in one direction, and then come back with the roundhouse from the other direction. It can be quite unexpected." This strategy could work with a hook kick to the head and roundhouse to the face, or hook kick to the head and roundhouse to the body, or even a hook kick to the back, drawing a person's guard to the rear in order to come back with a roundhouse to the solar plexus or stomach.

Fox says that double roundhouse kicks also work well because they're easy to perform and they can be done quickly. In this kind of double roundhouse combination, you kick and then touch the floor with your kicking foot before throwing the second kick. It's kick, touch, kick, touch.

Another kind of double roundhouse entails throwing the first kick, rechambering, and then throwing the second. Of course, in this combo, you don't touch the floor with the kicking leg before firing off the second kick. In both kinds of double roundhouses, the first kick isn't meant to do the damage. The second roundhouse is the weapon where you want most of your power and momentum. Your aim with a double roundhouse is to draw the opponent's guard away from the real target area. At a more advanced level, double roundhouse combos can become triples, and more—whatever it takes to get the opponent to either raise the arms, opening the abdomen, or lower the guard, opening the head to attack.

The weapon in an instep roundhouse kick is the talus (arrow), a large bone at the top of the ankle group.

A ball-of-the-foot roundhouse to the abdominal area or the ribs can be effective. This kick can wedge between an opponent's guard to strike the target.

Basics

There are effective jump roundhouse kicks as well, but Fox focuses on the basics with his students. "Adding a jump to a kick is like learning to use a weapon," Fox says. "You have to learn to use your hands effectively first before you add a more advanced weapon." For this reason, even Fox's advanced students also routinely practice and teach roundhouse kick basics.

"To execute a rear-leg roundhouse kick, begin in a fighting stance," Fox says. "Drawing the rear leg up, bring the knee high to a 45-degree angle pointing up and across the forward plane on the body, with the toes and foot pointing downward, preparing the instep weapon. This is the chamber. When the kick is executed, the extension of the kicking leg toward the target and the torque and twist of the hips happen at the same time."

It's important to perform the hip twist and snap out the kick at the same time. Then you return to chamber and either drop the leg where you want to or kick again. "It's important to chamber the roundhouse," Fox says. "Like a punch, if I draw my arm [straight] upward from my side and hit something with a straight arm, it'll actually only be a push. Chambering, cocking the arm, creates speed and snap, and that has a direct relationship to power. Similarly, if you eliminate the chamber the roundhouse kick can still be effective, as it can be using a straight-leg roundhouse, but you're not going to have that same driving force." Remember to hold the guard up and close to the body as you kick. Never let the arms flail.

Routines and Exercises

Fox uses a wealth of exercises and training routines to help his students develop their roundhouse kicks. "Bag work and shield work develop power," Fox says. "Pad work is best to develop focus on the smaller tar-

In this strength and technique drill, you face your partner and hold onto his or her shoulders. Slowly go through each step of the roundhouse kick. Then pump out five or ten fast kicks while still holding onto your partner.

get and speed. Pads are also useful for double-kick training. All these training aids can help develop distancing." Add these roundhouse kick drills and exercises to your training. Remember to work your roundhouses as front-leg and rear-leg kicks, and be sure to stretch properly before and after your workouts. (See Chapter 8 for more on warming up and stretching.)

Bag work

Use the bag to develop timing. As you kick the bag, it moves. Be sure to kick again as the bag moves back into position, as an opponent would. Remember to position yourself so that you are throwing your kicks through the target, not just hitting the front of the bag.

In a tension kicking drill, hold onto a bar or chair back and slowly execute each step of the roundhouse kick.

A shield is a vital part of a power drill. One person holds the shield and moves around. The other person follows, kicking.

Two-Person Reaction Drill

Fox uses this drill to sharpen reaction time and speed. Face off with a partner. As your partner throws a roundhouse, you block and immediately return with a roundhouse. Your partner does the same. It's touch, kick, touch, kick—fast. "This exercise helps you learn to keep your guard up while fighting, and it helps students remember proper form when kicking," Fox says.

Speed Drill

The instructor holds a shield as two students, one on the instructor's left, the other on his right, alternately kick. As soon as your partner kicks and drops the leg, you kick the shield. Like the two-person reaction drill, this speed drill is very demanding but very practical for developing speed and technique.

Power Drill

The instructor holds a shield, but only one person kicks. The instructor moves around, and the student follows, kicking. Let each kick in this drill generate maximum power. Fox uses this drill to teach students the most effective angle from which to throw a roundhouse. "This drill is especially useful if you're in a situation where you need to execute one fast, strong technique either to drop an attacker or score a point," Fox says.

Skipping Drill

Keep the leg chambered and hop the length of the training area, kicking as you go. Fox uses this drill to help students develop balance and control. "In point competition this kind of kicking can be useful against someone who often moves backward," Fox says. "You keep flicking that kick as you follow the opponent's retreat."

Strength and Technique Drill

Face your partner and hold onto his or her arms and shoulders. Slowly go through each step of executing the roundhouse kick. Then pump out 5 or 10 fast kicks while still holding onto your partner. "This drill is painful and difficult, but it's one of the best partner drills to develop strength and proper technique for this kick," Fox says.

Tension Kicking

Hold onto a bar or chair back and slowly execute each step of the roundhouse kick. Be meticulous about positioning and laying out the kick very slowly. This drill, like the one before, is excellent for building strength and technique.

Pad work is useful in developing speed and focus on the smaller target. Pads are also useful for double-kick training.

Back-and-Forth Combinations Drill

With a partner who just defends, you kick. The defender shuffles backward and moves around to create different angles so that you have to reposition your body to kick. This drill lets you work on your distancing and angling.

Muscle Dynamics

"The key muscles for executing roundhouse kicks, as well as side kicks and hook kicks, are the hip flexors," Fox says. "The stronger and more developed your hip flexors are, the more powerful your kicks will be, and the more control you'll have." The driving muscles are the quadriceps and the hamstrings. The twisting motion inherent in a powerful roundhouse kick means that the abdominals and lower back muscles should also be developed.

Train hard to develop your roundhouse kicks. In class, in competition, and on the street, let these versatile weapons work for you.

Art Michaels is a Harrisburg, Pennsylvania–based freelance writer and Tae Kwon Do black belt. This material originally appeared in the June 1995 issue of Inside Tae Kwon Do *magazine.*

17

Side Kick Basics

Art Michaels

It's amazing how effective basic techniques can be. The side kick, a Tae Kwon Do trademark, is one such fundamental technique. When executed correctly in the appropriate circumstance, it can be remarkably practical and decisive.

The side kick, a Tae Kwon Do trademark, can be an exceptionally devastating weapon when it's executed properly.

You and your wife take turns pushing a stroller along a crowded boardwalk. Your year-old son chews on a toy, oblivious to the noise, lights, people, and distant surf. Suddenly from the crowd a man careens backward and falls, slamming his left shoulder into the wheel of your child's stroller. The stroller lurches sideways and your son cries. He is frightened but otherwise unharmed. The man stands slowly, and is clearly intoxicated.

The man turns toward your wife. He puts his arm around her and mumbles an obscenity. Instantly she slams her elbow into his ribs. He buckles sideways. Shouting more obscenities he lurches toward her, his hands reaching for her throat. She rivets a front-leg side kick squarely into the attacker's solar plexus. He collapses backward, this time into the arms of two police officers.

As this scenario illustrates, a well-executed basic side kick can have rewarding results. "The side kick is a Tae Kwon Do trademark," says Master Joe Fox of the Harrisburg, Pennsylvania, Institute of Tae Kwon Do, "and it can work for you high or low, no matter how flexible—or inflexible—you are. But to maximize the kick's effectiveness, you have to execute it properly."

Concentrated Kicking Drill

Fox teaches the side kick in a "concentrated kicking" drill, which he says is one of the most important side kick training exercises. "Many people who are not especially flexible try to compensate for the lack of flexibility when they throw a side kick by leaning the body down and thrusting the leg as high as they can," Fox says. "The more you lean downward, the less power you have at the end of the kick, where you

The concentrated side kick drill divides the kick into slow-moving parts. Hold each part about three seconds. Begin in a fighting stance.

Bring the rear leg into a snap kick chamber. This initial movement rotates the hips to face the target.

Turn the hips to a side position and hold the leg in this side kick chamber. At this point, the kicking foot should be in a knifelike position with the toes up.

Extend the kick. The heel of the kicking foot should be in a straight line with the shoulders and hips.

want the power to be greatest. On the other hand, many agile people don't develop their side kicks to the level they could because they're very flexible and they can shoot their legs up very high. In both cases, breaking down the details of positioning the body, chambering, and foot placement can help anyone develop a side kick—low, midlevel, or high—that is an extremely devastating and effective weapon. The kick's snap and speed are the main ingredients in how powerful the side kick is, but unless the kick is executed correctly, it will be lacking."

Fox's concentrated kicking drill includes five steps that divide the side kick into slow-moving parts. Begin in a fighting stance.

1. Bring the rear leg into a snap kick chamber. This initial movement rotates the hips to face the target.
2. Turn the hips to a side position and hold the leg in this side kick chamber. At this point, the kicking foot should be in a knifelike position with the toes up.
3. Extend the kick. The heel of the kicking foot should be in a straight line with the shoulders and hips. This position lets you bring your full body weight to bear into the kick, maximizing your kick's power.
4. Rechamber the kick.
5. Place the leg down again, returning to the fighting stance.

"Practicing this drill repeatedly is much more important than shooting out fast side kicks all the time," Fox says. "Slow, concentrated kicking develops all the muscles used to throw the side kick, and it helps students keep their balance during the kick. If you maintain your balance during concentrated kicking, you can keep it when you execute a side kick fast because your momentum is much greater."

Fox says it's essential when you execute a side kick full speed that all the correct steps are there. Practicing the concentrated side kick drill lets you

develop all the detail in the side kick naturally, so you don't have to think about each step when you kick at full speed and power.

One common mistake, Fox notes, is throwing a side kick and striking the target with the flat part of the foot instead of the blade of the foot near the heel. He likens this mistake to slapping someone instead of hitting with the knuckles of a tightly clenched fist—

Master Joe Fox (left) checks Dustin Smith's side kick position. Note that Smith's guard is up. The support leg is pointed almost in the opposite direction of the kick, opening the hips.

not bringing one's full power to bear. "During the side kick, the foot of the support leg should point in the opposite direction of the kick so that the hips open," Fox says. "Some people who are extremely flexible can execute an effective side kick with proper form without turning the plant foot. However, most people must open the hips to get the full power, so it's important to turn the support foot in the opposite direction of the kick."

Keep the Guard Up

Fox also teaches students to keep the guard up—hold the hands up and in with tightly clenched fists. He stresses that if your side kick is blocked, you can expect an immediate counter. If you throw your

The attacker (left) attempts a reverse punch. In this defense, the defender plants a side kick just above the attacker's knee.

arms out with the kick, or if you let your arms drop, your body and face are exposed and you have no defense. "Some students are taught to maintain balance while kicking by extending the arms, as if they were on a balance beam," Fox says. "I teach students right from the start to keep the guard up. When you train throwing a side kick with the guard up and in, your balance develops with that position. If you throw your arms out to maintain balance when you kick, when you try keeping the guard up and in, you'll be very unsteady. If you learn right from the start to keep the guard up when you kick, as your kicks go higher you can maintain your balance without throwing the arms out. The height of your kicks will increase, and you maintain the kick's effectiveness and power as your flexibility and strength

increase. The height, effectiveness, and power of the side kick will not grow from forcing the kick up and using your arms to keep from falling."

Fox encourages his students to work with one another, with a bag, and with a mirror. Fox says that bag training helps develop one's power. "You can exe-

The attacker (right) attempts a front snap kick, but the defender counters with a powerful side kick to the attacker's stomach.

cute full power and full focus when you kick a bag. This gives you an idea of how strong your side kick is, and knowing what your side kick can actually do increases your confidence." Training with a bag or with a partner also teaches distancing. If you're too close, you jam the kick, and if you don't chamber properly, you can't hit the target effectively. Fox also encourages his students to work in front of a mirror so that they see correct form, and repeat it as they practice.

Street Application

"On the street, the most practical application of a side kick is to pick a target from the ribs downward,

A knife-wielding assailant attempts a thrust. The defender lands a side kick just above the attacker's hip flexor.

Fox says. "When the snap kick is thrown, the body twists forward, and with a driving side kick, you can use the attacker's forward momentum again to increase your side kick's effectiveness. When someone executes a technique—a punch or a kick—the stomach muscles loosen slightly. If you catch an attacker at this point with a side kick to the stomach, it's easier to stop him."

The attacker tries a backfist or jab. The defender takes advantage of the attacker's forward momentum and rivets a side kick just below the attacker's ninth rib—the solar plexus area.

depending on how much danger you're in," Fox says. "If you feel you must immobilize an attacker, go for just above the knee." Fox says another target is right above the hip flexor. There's a sensitive pressure point there, and hitting it with a side kick can cause a person to drop. A strike there is painful, but landing a side kick there won't cause lasting damage.

"You can incapacitate a person with a side kick to the ribs," Fox says, "but this is a good example of why snapping, chambering, and foot position—striking with the blade of the foot near the heel—are so important. You're using the attacker's forward momentum and shooting the side kick right below the ninth rib—the solar plexus." This hard strike, when properly executed, drives the diaphragm upward, knocking the wind out of an attacker. The jolt to the diaphragm makes it temporarily difficult to move air into the lungs.

"A side kick to the stomach is a useful defense against someone attacking with a front snap kick,"

The sport application of the side kick is the same as the street application, except that you don't target below the waist and you execute the kick with control. In street defense, the higher you kick the less power you have, unless you're very flexible, and the more vulnerable you are to a counterattack," Fox says. "For this reason, an important element to consider is the environment. Are you standing on a flat surface, on an incline, on gravel, stone, ice, water, snow, grass? That's why the street application of the side kick is best from the ribs downward. Depending on what you're standing on and where you are, you might slip."

Fox focuses on the side kick because it can be so effective both in self-defense and in competition. If you take a closer look at how you execute this basic technique and apply these ideas, you could hone Tae Kwon Do's trademark into an exceptionally devastating weapon.

Art Michaels is a Harrisburg, Pennsylvania—based freelance writer and a Tae Kwon Do black belt. This material originally appeared in the April 1994 issue of Inside Tae Kwon Do *magazine.*

18

Putting Power Behind the Side Kick

Terry Brumley

Make these minor adjustments, asserts the author, and you can gain tremendous power and accuracy in your side kick. Furthermore, throwing the side kick properly will promote longevity in your training instead of hampering your performance with unnecessary injuries.

While living in Birmingham, Alabama, I was associated with a martial arts school where all of the instructors and black belts complained about pain in their knees, especially after a class drilling the side kick. One evening, after a black belt workout, all of the men hit the odorous locker room. Almost everyone was benched holding their knees. One second-degree black belt moaned, "I must not be built right to be a martial artist." Several other moaners agreed. I said, "You're not built to hyperextend your knees." By the glares and grimaces, I realized that I was treading on thin ice. The moaner growled, "I do what the Master says!" I stood and said, "I know, and his knees hurt too." The pain-stricken moaners stood up, and I realized that I had broken through the thin ice and was sinking.

I was lucky enough to have a few wise instructors in the beginning of my training who understood the physiological and kinesthetic makeup of the body and how it worked. The tide is changing in the martial arts industry. Twenty years ago, most black belt instructors received very limited training on the correct way to deliver a movement. By correct, I mean a technique that delivers maximum power with the least energy and the least wear and tear on the muscles and skeletal structure. Nowadays, many instructors are well versed in the professional approach that will develop greater longevity in the martial arts. This chapter will teach you how to develop a powerful side kick that will be healthy to practice for many happy martial arts years to come.

Breaking Down the Stationary Side Kick

In teaching the side kick, we will study the stationary side kick. These mechanics can be applied to the spin, turning, jumping, or any other side kick. I have broken down its delivery into four steps: the pivot, the chamber, firing, and retraction.

Step One: The Pivot

The main reason to pivot is to place the hips in the correct alignment to correctly chamber the kick. The standing foot should pivot either on the ball of the foot or in the air. Pivoting on the ball of your foot is considerably faster than flat-footed pivoting. Also, it takes the pressure off your knee that usually results from flat-footed pivoting. Fastest, but most difficult, is pivoting in the air. After you have mastered the pivot in the air, you will never go back to the flat-footed pivot. (A flat-footed pivot means pivoting on the ball of the foot while the heel is having some contact with the floor. Just because you have an arch and are not completely flat-footed does not mean you may not be pivoting flat-footed.)

The foot should pivot until the stationary heel is pointing toward the target. Most martial artists do not pivot this far. When you pivot to point the heel at the target, the hips are aligned to gain a full correct chamber. Anything less results in a weak, ineffective, incorrect leg-slinging exercise that should not be categorized as a side kick.

Step Two: The Chamber

This brings us to our second step: the chamber. The chamber is the cocked and ready-to-fire position. An effective chamber is one that raises the knee and foot as high as possible, as flat as possible, and as close to the chest as possible without compromising your posture.

Some say, "Only raise the knee and foot as high as you kick." I disagree. Gravity is our friend. Let's call on its help as often as possible. I can always kick down and low if necessary. But the problem with most martial artists is not the inability to kick low; it's the inability to kick high. The higher the chamber, the better the chance for developing a higher side kick.

The knee and foot should also be as flat as possible, as if you were laying your knee and foot across a table. The more level the foot is, the straighter the kick will travel to the target. This will provide more power. The knee pushes the foot to the target on the side kick. If the foot is too high or too low, the more the knee has to work for the same results. The flatter the better.

The knee-to-the-chest theory is based on a slingshot. Pull it halfway back and the rock travels half of its flying potential. Don't blame it on the rock—it just wasn't pulled back as far as it should have been. A full-chambered side kick is almost as fast as a half-chambered side kick but twice as powerful. You weigh the difference.

Now, this is where many martial artists miss out: *The full pivot and full chamber must be completed at the same exact time.* If not, the whole side kick will suffer. If the pivot reaches completion first, the side kick chamber fires before chamber completion. When the chamber reaches completion first, the pivot normally stops. The kick fires prematurely, causing the foot to chase the target since the knee and foot were never in line with the target. Either way, you produce an inferior side kick. When the pivot and chamber complete simultaneously, the side kick has a much greater chance of maximum power. Many martial artists will chamber first, and then pivot at the very end of the kick for added power. The problems with this are angle and hyperextension. The knee and heel cannot be in the correct line with the target if the foot is not correctly and fully pivoted. This off-angle kick produces less power. In archery, by analogy, a straight arrow has to be pulled back straight to fly straight to the target. The same goes for the side kick. Hyperextension normally comes from the knee traveling in a direction other than the heel. This is very common when a pivot is part of the end of the kick rather than part of the chamber.

Step Three: Firing

When firing, we have to remember two key concepts: power and accuracy. This section covers both.

If you remember anything about this segment, remember this: push the knee, not the foot, to the target. Many side kicks start off correctly, but lose power at the end for this very reason. If the knee gets off-target and, instead of correcting the knee, you allow the foot to jump in to save the day and make the adjustment to the target, you lose power. The knee needs to travel to and fro many times until it can become accurate. This will fix the loss of power and improve accuracy.

The eyes must stay on the target throughout the kick. Failure to do this is the biggest reason for inaccuracy. Even Kwai Chang Caine (David Carradine) in the original *Kung Fu* TV series kept his eyes open while trying to snag the pebbles from the Master's hand. And did you notice that the Master kept his eyes open too? Focus on the center of the target. Just like in darts. Don't focus on the dart-board, focus on the bulls-eye. Your side kick might not hit the bull's-eye every time, but if the focus is accurate, you will avoid missing the whole dartboard!

In using these tools to re-create a more accurate, more powerful side kick, remember the lesson I learned as a child. My goal as a child was to go squirrel hunting with my father and big brother. So, after extensive begging on my part, my father struck a deal with me. "When you can hit ten cans at twenty paces with 100-percent accuracy," he said, "then you can go squirrel hunting." After spending many cases

of .22 shells, the time had come. I was accurate at twenty paces with a non-moving target. To my surprise, squirrels were like sparring partners. They didn't stand still while I fired at them!

Step Four: Retraction

The final step in the side kick is the retraction or recoil. Recoil the kick back into its chambered position. There is a lot of controversy between the masters on this segment. Some say, "Retract evenly for a side, roundhouse or hook kick." Some say, "A half retraction is best because you can attack faster, plus your balance is better." I favor a full retraction that replicates the chamber to a *T*. There are not enough correct side kick chambers out there; the chamber needs as much practice as possible. A full retraction will result in two full chambers per kick. This will develop your side kick twice as fast. My next justification for full retraction is preparation. If you are doing a side kick/roundhouse kick combination, you should retract as for a roundhouse kick. But if you are not sure what kick you will do after a side kick, then retract for a side kick. It's more powerful than a hook or a roundhouse and it will create distance between you and your opponent.

Practice these principles of the side kick and you will develop both power and accuracy when executing this fundamental kick.

Terry Brumley owns and operates the Tae Kwon Do University in Memphis, Tennessee. He and his instructors use martial arts as a vehicle for teaching self-esteem, discipline, and confidence, as well as physical fitness and self-defense. This material originally appeared in the September 1995 issue of Inside Tae Kwon Do *magazine.*

19

Tae Kwon Do's 360-Degree Jumping Roundhouse Kick

Jane Hallander

The combination of three different kicks, 360–degree jumping roundhouse kicks operate on the premise that the first two kicks are fakes and the third scores the point. Here we answer the question "Why use such an intricate technique, when a single kick might achieve the same results?"

Three-hundred-sixty-degree jumping round-house kicks are surprise techniques designed to take opponents off balance and score quick points. They work because the opponent doesn't know for sure what will happen after you start your turn. They are also distance-covering techniques, allowing fighters to charge forward, launching a big surprise for the opponent.

San Rafael, California—based Tae Kwon Do instructor Ali Alamulhuda knows the value of 360-degree roundhouse kicks. He's been using them successfully throughout the 25 years that he has taught Tae Kwon Do. Alamulhuda has personally won many championships in both Tae Kwon Do and open martial arts tournaments. His students follow in his footsteps, winning at large American and international tournaments, such as the Asian Championships.

"The 360-degree jumping roundhouse technique is actually the result of three separate roundhouse kicks," explains Alamulhuda. "The first is a low, knee-to-groin-level kick. The second is a middle-distance technique. Finally, the 360-degree roundhouse kick follows. Tactically, the first two kicks are faking techniques, making the 360-degree kick the scoring technique." Many Tae Kwon Do competitors use 360-degree roundhouse kicks as single techniques, not realizing that faking kicks and the resulting combinations are far more effective than single techniques. They just start kicking, without regard to target or strategy.

The 360-degree jumping roundhouse kicks can be done either clockwise or counterclockwise. Performing them requires flexibility and the ability to jump straight up in the air, simultaneously turning

360 degrees. Since 360-degree kicks are distance-covering techniques, they are usually executed from several steps away from the opponent. He may be retreating from the kicker. Also, the 360-degree kick may follow a faking ploy in which the kicker appears to be retreating, but is actually setting his opponent up for a surprise 360-degree kick.

Follow the Eyes

From the start of the kick until its conclusion, never take your eyes off the opponent. Your body turns, but your eyes should remain directed toward the opponent. Three-hundred-sixty-degree jumping roundhouse kicks can be dangerous techniques if your opponent rushes forward and jams your kick. For that reason, it's essential that you keep your eyes on your opponent at all times. Not easy kicks, 360-degree roundhouse kicks require flexibility, a good warm-up, and light, fast footwork. They are not white-belt-level kicks.

Using it as a combination technique, the Tae Kwon Do stylist starts with a low faking back-leg kick toward the opponent's groin area. To make it a faking technique, Alamulhuda kicks, then lets his kicking leg drop slightly downward. Right before it moves back into the original stance position, he throws another roundhouse, with the same foot, to the opponent's stomach. Most adept opponents will successfully block the first two kicks. What the opponent cannot block is the next kick—the 360-degree jumping roundhouse kick. Alamulhuda puts his kicking leg down on the ground, immediately jumping into a 360-degree roundhouse with the same leg.

The Power to Intimidate

The 360-degree roundhouse kick can be used whenever you have a good target. It's a good technique to start with as an aggressive attack. These kicks intimidate opponents with their speed and power. They are forward-moving kicks, used against close-range opponents. The 360-degree jumping roundhouse is not a retreating kick technique.

Since it is a jumping technique aimed at high targets, such as the opponent's head, it is a perfect kick for Tae Kwon Do tournaments, where competitors can score points by kicking their opponent's face. Because it takes three to four seconds to turn and requires good flexibility, Alamalhuda does not recommend 360-degree jumping roundhouse kicks for self-defense. Since you don't have much choice in advance whether you wear loose or tight clothes for your street self-defense, jumping kicks work only if the timing and circumstances are just right. You cannot ask your attacker to wait a minute while you warm up. Also, any jumping kick is risky in street-fighting situations. When you are off the ground, you are vulnerable to a sudden takedown. Hitting the ground could knock you unconscious or place you in a position with your attacker on top and in control. For self-defense, Alamalhuda recommends lower, basic kicks, such as side or stationary roundhouse kicks.

Mastering the Kick

Good 360-degree jumping roundhouse kicks start by developing the three kicks (low, middle, and jumping 360-degree roundhouses) individually, until you are good enough at all three to adjust your movement and timing into the combination kick.

Alamalhuda then starts his students on combinations with just the first two kicks, using two students against each other. When they master the two-kick combination, he adds the "360" to finish the combination. They train against body shields and focus pads, never with heavy hanging bags, because they need a moving target for the light, speedy 360-degree roundhouse. Heavy bags are too rigid, stopping your power and slowing your footwork. Alamalhuda also warns not to train too much in the air, without a target. You need a target to develop control and accuracy. Training only in the air could also lead to knee or hip injuries from overextending the joints—a target stops their extension. You need a target to see the effects of your kicking power. The 360-degree jumping roundhouse is famous as a breaking technique, and practicing it by breaking boards develops power, speed, and accuracy.

This kick requires thorough warming up and stretching. The lower body, especially the waist and hips, are most important to stretch and warm up. Front stretch kicks and gentle warm-ups with ankle weights are recommended. However, don't try any of the three kicks (especially the jumping roundhouse) while wearing ankle weights—it's too hard on knee, ankle, and hip joints. Alamalhuda encourages his students to develop kicking height and leg strength by practicing lifting kicks, above head level.

Always land with the kicking foot forward, since the next technique might be a spinning hook kick or a back kick with the other leg. Remember, the key to all successful combinations, like the 360-degree jumping roundhouse, is speed and a firm commitment to each kick. Any hesitation telegraphs to your opponent that you are susceptible to a jamming technique and counterattack.

Jane Hallander is a veteran martial arts writer and a regular contributor to CFW Enterprises publications. This material originally appeared in the April 1994 issue of Inside Tae Kwon Do *magazine.*

20

Flying Kicks

How and Why You Can Make Them Work

Andre Alex Lima

Let's face it, when it comes right down to naming the most spectacular techniques in the entire martial arts spectrum, nothing beats Tae Kwon Do's flamboyant flying kicks. Practical or not, when flying kicks are done well they represent the athletic pinnacle of the martial arts. Here are some provocative insights into aerial artistry from a Tae Kwon Do champion who practices what he preaches.

It's a fact that Tae Kwon Do flying kicks and other techniques that require the martial artist to leap before delivering are spectacular and the absolute favorite among the general public. They deserve to be seen again in slow motion and, once seen, are not likely to be forgotten.

More than any other single technique, the flying kick is associated with Tae Kwon Do and has drawn the public to this Korean martial art. Consequently, Tae Kwon Do has enjoyed rapid and remarkable growth and is now quite possibly the world's most popular martial art. Granted, the throws of judo and aikido, and some of the more sophisticated techniques of other arts and styles, are equally spectacular. But nothing more perfectly defines fancy or sensational like a flamboyant flying kick. It is my intention to simplify and structure these flying kicks

so that every reader, regardless of his or her style, can learn to perform these acrobatic techniques.

Historical Origins in the Orient

The exact origins of flying kicks are lost in the mysticism of the ancient Orient. Historians believe that these techniques were first developed at the Shaolin temple in China, and then taken to other parts of the Orient. There is no doubt that such techniques were used and developed with greater intensity in Korea. Almost all styles of fighting from this country have a vast arsenal of flying kicks, including Tae Kwon Do, Hapkido, Hwarang-do, Kuk Sool Won, and others. Undoubtedly, Korea is the world capital for flying kicks, and Tae Kwon Do is the martial art that boasts the most complete arsenal of these techniques. The Korean terminology for jumps is *timio* or *tuio*.

The first historical evidence proving the practice of such techniques in the past was found in 1935 by a group of Japanese archaeologists led by Tadashi Saito. Saito and his staff wrote *Study of Ancient Korean Culture*, which is to this day considered one of the definitive works on this subject. Citing ancient documents, the book dates flying kicks back to the beginning of the Koryo Dynasty, founded in 918 B.C. One such document says that a "style of fight developed by local priests helped its practitioners to become agile, swift specialists in movements of defense" and that they "attack with flying kicks." This declaration was found in the files of a temple called "Kwon Bup." Through unknown and undocumented development, these techniques were progressively refined, passing from master to student for centuries, arriving in modern times as the most spectacular part of the martial arts.

Popularization in Hollywood

From their origin in Asia, flying kicks were transmitted to the West by Asian immigrants and then, surprisingly early, found their way to a cursory application in motion picture fight scenes. Thanks to the movies, it wasn't long before they were popularized worldwide. The first person to apply them effectively on film was Bruce Lee, who immortalized the image of the flying side kick, today the most well-known traditional technique in the aerial kick arsenal.

Subsequently, many other actors began to use the same technique in order to attract ever-bigger movie audiences. The more spectacular and explosive the jump kicks are on screen, the more animated the audience becomes. Art Camacho, one of Hollywood's foremost fight choreographers, with more than twenty-five film credits, says, "An actor, in order to be successful nowadays in the martial arts, has to be able to perform difficult and acrobatic techniques, especially jump kicks, which may not be useful in a real situation, but are for sure the favorite of the public."

Benny "The Jet" Urquidez, another choreographer of martial arts movies and a legendary kickboxing champion, says, "We normally choreograph the decisive fights in movies in a special way. We first make the actors exchange a series of simple and easy strikes. After that, for the final strike—the one which defines the fight—we generally use a jump kick to the head to be spectacular. " In the 1970s, a huge quantity of inexpensively-produced martial arts movies in which directors and choreographers used lots of jump and acrobatic techniques was produced in Hong Kong. Some experts in this subject think that by using too many of these techniques a movie loses its emotion and becomes boring. However, box-office earnings from Hollywood martial arts movies tell a very different story. When it comes to spectacular action scenes, in the West, more is definitely better.

The Efficiency Debate

Many black belts and masters from all different styles perform jump kicks in public demonstrations. These kicks impress viewers and attract new students to the practice of martial arts. However, opinions about such techniques vary significantly, especially regarding efficiency. A good number of fighters—generally from styles that do not use many jump techniques—criticize these techniques and discourage their students from using them. Says one, "Jump kicks are not efficient for self-defense. They are difficult to perform and totally impossible for street fights!" Others say that scoring points in competition with a jump kick is a "lucky shot." Trying to score this way represents a big risk, they maintain. "You can lose balance," says one critic, "and besides, the strikes get weaker when the user is in the air, without at least one foot firmly planted on the floor."

Nevertheless, Tae Kwon Do masters, some known as "jump kick masters," have a very different opinion. Claims one such master, "The ones who criticize jump-kick techniques are generally those who never learned to perform them, and it is not right to give an opinion about something one does not know how to do." Famous Tae Kwon Do master Hee Il Cho, who does use flying kicks, once said, "I have used these techniques all my life, so I should know, and I say they are very efficient and powerful and can be used in any kind of situation—demonstrations, competitions, and even in a street fight for self-defense. Any technique has efficiency if one practices it frequently!"

Technical Aspects

Practically all kicking techniques can be performed with a jump, causing a considerable increase of reach not only in height but also in distance, as well as an increase in power. Jumping front kicks are simpler and easier to perform than other jumping kicks because they don't require hip rotation, yet they still increase a kick's power. On the other hand, the kicks that require hip rotation in the air are more difficult, but, when executed correctly, can be amazingly powerful.

Jumps may be used to either attack or counterattack. However, when defending oneself in a street fight, one must be cautious when using the jump techniques with rotation because one "offers" one's back to the opponent.

The major function of training "in the air" (without a target) or in front of a mirror is to master the movement. Many less-experienced athletes make the mistake of telegraphing to opponents their intention to perform the jump—many times with arm movement, as if to gain propulsion for the jump. This robs technique of the critical element of surprise.

To jump with maximum power, one must use gravity by jumping a little higher than (or at least the same height as) the intended target so the downward motion of the body helps in the process. If the body stays below the target, the kick will be performed upward with only the help of the leg once the body weight, by gravity, drops its force downward.

Types of Jumps

There are two distinct types of jumping techniques: flying kick and jump kicks. The difference is the way one makes use of them. The jump kick is used at close range, with the fighter jumping directly into a kick on the intended target. It may be used for attack or counterattack and it is performed practically in place from start to finish. The flying kick is used with the intent to cover some distance, with the athlete remaining in the air for some time before executing the kick. Generally, the athlete tries to fly over an obstacle or barrier, hitting the target at the other side (or at the end of this obstacle or barrier). It is exclusively a technique for attack.

Simple, Double, and Triple Jumps—and Beyond

Simple Jumps: Those in which the athlete kicks just once while in the air. They are divided into three kinds: direct, spinning, and lever.

Direct: Those kicks wherein the foot goes directly to the target, describing a nearly straight line in its trajectory.

Spinning: In these kicks, the foot describes a circle or semicircle in its trajectory from the floor to the target.

Lever: These kicks consist of lifting one of the knees as a lever in order to get more propulsion behind the kicking leg. Often used for teaching beginners, they

are easy and have a mechanism that allows great power and speed.

Double jumps: Those in which the athlete kicks twice in the air before landing. They are subdivided in "simultaneous" and "alternate."

Simultaneous: As the name implies, the athlete kicks in the air with both legs at the same time, at just one target or two different targets. These kicks are typically used for demonstrations, and they require a good deal of physical preparation.

Alternate: Many times the first of these two kicks executed one after the other works as a fake move for the second one, which, because of the lever used, is usually stronger than the first one. These kicks may be used in competition.

Triple-plus jumps: These techniques were developed strictly for demonstrations. The athlete jumps and performs in the air three, four, or more kicks before landing. They require excellent physical preparation and a lot of practice time.

The Three Parts of a Jump Kick

Propulsion

The leg musculature must exert enough power to thrust the body into the air for the period of time necessary to the kick. Propulsion can be achieved in three ways: from a standing position, with previous steps, or with an initial run. From a standing position, one typically thrusts with both legs. When in motion, one usually performs the final thrust with

one of the legs, while coming off the final step. Propulsion is the part of the flying kick that consumes the most energy.

Flight

A difficult and complex part! It requires a lot of agility and coordination on the part of the athlete, who must be able to improvise a fall if he or she loses balance or makes an error in the moment of execution. One must also be prepared to adjust the distance in case the target moves, which is likely. During the flight one must have perfect timing and must keep the upper body as vertical as possible.

Fall

The fall adjustment must be steady and precise, or the whole jump process will be damaged. In the majority of cases, one foot will touch the floor before the other. Some masters teach their students to land with both feet at the same time; they believe this is the safest way to land and the best way to avoid any unbalance.

Andre Alex Lima of Venice, California, is a retired European Tae Kwon Do heavyweight champion and one of the world's leading martial arts freelance writers. His articles have appeared in martial arts magazines throughout the world in various languages. This material originally appeared in the December 1994 issue of Inside Tae Kwon Do *magazine.*

21

Tae Kwon Do's Deadly Groin Kicks

Attacking and Defending a Vital Area

Art Michaels

In real self-defense, the groin appears to be an obvious target, but it isn't an easy spot to hit squarely. The groin is actually a small target, and an attacker usually moves constantly. So, abruptly ending a confrontation with a shot aimed at the groin isn't a certainty. Groin strikes do work, but you have to strike accurately, powerfully, and quickly.

These basic Tae Kwon Do techniques can be used to guard against groin strikes: (left to right) a low pressing block, down block, low knife-hand block, and chambering a leg.

In some traditional Tae Kwon Do forms, low blocks, low knife-hand blocks, and low pressing blocks can be interpreted as defenses against groin strikes. Other forms that Tae Kwon Do stylists practice, including Chong Moo, Koryo, Bassai, and Kanku, contain *sudo* (open-hand) groin strikes and groin-tearing techniques.

The powerful beginning movement of Bassai—lowering the two hands directly in front of the body—can be interpreted as a pressing block, defending against a groin strike. Bassai also includes chambering a leg to protect the groin from a kick, as do the forms Pyung Idan and Pyung Samdan. This long history of practicing groin strikes and blocks in forms suggests that over the centuries, no one had to tell martial artists that the groin is a vital self-defense target, and that attackers would attempt groin strikes.

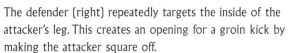

The defender (right) repeatedly targets the inside of the attacker's leg. This creates an opening for a groin kick by making the attacker square off.

As the attacker squares off, the defender follows immediately with a mule (heel) kick to the exposed groin.

Although the groin appears to be an obvious target, it isn't such an easy spot to hit squarely. The groin is actually a small target, and an attacker usually moves constantly. Unless an attacker stands still in an open stance, connecting with a groin shot that abruptly ends a confrontation isn't a certainty. Furthermore, the adrenalin that flows during a fight lets some people continue even after taking an apparently well-placed groin kick or punch. This is especially true when an attacker is under the influence of drugs that suppress pain. Groin strikes can be practical, and they should certainly be part of your self-defense repertoire. But to be effective, groin strikes require precision, skill, and lots of practice.

The defender (right) creates another opening for a groin strike by making the attacker square off. First, the defender strikes the back of the leg with a series of roundhouse kicks.

The attacker begins to square off as he moves the leg backward in reaction to the painful roundhouse kicks. The defender follows the last roundhouse kick immediately with a hook kick to the inside of the attacker's leg, making the attacker square off further.

The defender follows the hook kick immediately with a mule (heel) kick to the attacker's exposed groin.

Setting Up the Attacker

"To set up a groin strike, if the attacker chooses not to wrestle you to the ground, you must make the attacker square off, or create your own opening that exposes the attacker's groin," says Joe Fox, a Harrisburg, Pennsylvania–based Tae Kwon Do instructor. "Hard roundhouse kicks to the back of the leg can cause an attacker to start twisting toward the pain to protect the leg. This squares the attacker's body to you and opens the groin area to your attack.

"When an attacker squares off to you, an effective technique is a hard, thrusting front snap kick," Fox says. Even if you don't connect, the power of the kick might still cause a lot of pain in the lower abdomen. The lower abdominal area just above the groin is a difficult area to condition, so a hard kick there could help you set up an attacker for another strike, or it might give you the opportunity to retreat. "When an attacker squares off to deliver a punch or a kick, a straight lifting kick with the instep might also be effective," Fox says.

The snap kick and the straight lifting kick can work with either the front leg or the rear leg, but you need speed and accuracy to execute these kicks effectively during that brief moment when the attacker squares off to you. If the attacker is positioned in a side-fighting stance, somewhat protecting the groin, a very hard ball-of-the-foot roundhouse kick to the groin might also work.

"Another way to create an open groin shot is to target the inner thigh of one leg with an instep roundhouse kick," Fox says. "During the instant the attacker squares off to you after you've delivered the roundhouse, rechamber the kick and follow immediately with a mule kick [heel] to the groin." Fox says that an experienced defender could also move under an attacker who tries a high kick, throwing a side kick to the attacker's groin.

As you practice groin attacks and combinations that lead to groin strikes, don't think that the defense finishes with the groin shot. Train to include other

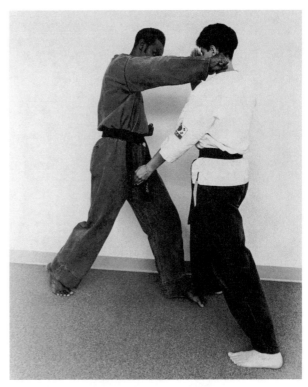

This technique appears in several traditional Tae Kwon Do forms. The defender (right) blocks the attacker's punch and counters with a sudo groin strike.

techniques after you've delivered a groin strike. For example, if you move under a high kick and execute a side kick to the attacker's groin, you might continue with another groin strike, target the attacker's knee, or execute a takedown. Hands aren't usually the weapon used in groin strikes. However, if an attacker throws a high kick and you have enough experience and speed, you can block, go under the kick, and strike the groin with a hand technique.

Similarly, if an attacker attempts a side kick, evade the kick by moving sideways. Then, as you trap the kicking leg, strike the attacker's exposed groin with a palm heel or a ridgehand. A similar defense appears in the traditional Tae Kwon Do form Pyung Odon. With your left hand, you block a left-leg roundhouse kick to the right side of your face while executing a right-hand fingertip knifehand strike to the attacker's groin. You could apply a similar response to a punch. As you block a right-hand punch

The defender (left) steps out of the way of the attacker's side kick. The defender traps the leg and strikes the attacker's groin with a sudo strike.

with your left hand, with your right hand strike the groin with a ridgehand or palm heel. This is Miyagi's technique in *The Karate Kid, Part II*, when he wards off the first of three attackers. You could also block the kick or punch, grab the shoulder and back of the neck, draw the attacker down and into a knee strike to the groin.

Protecting the Groin

"Someone who goes for the groin is usually the defender, not the attacker," Fox says. "Attackers usually go for the head or the body, or the attacker tries to take you to the ground. Nevertheless, protecting the groin is still vital." The key to protecting the groin is not to square off to an attacker. When you are confronted by an attacker who chooses not to grapple right away, remain in a side stance, fighting stance, or even a more traditional Tae Kwon Do back stance so that the attacker cannot easily strike your groin.

"You should keep the guard up to protect both sides of the face. That means keeping the fists tight and up. To protect both sides of the body, keep the

elbows in close to the ribs," Fox says. "An attacker will likely go for your body or your knees. With training and experience, you maneuver so you don't give an attacker a clean knee strike or open shot to your groin, and your hands guard the head and upper body.

"In point fighting, I fight with one hand protecting the face and one hand down protecting the groin," Fox says. "In competition, an opponent isn't coming at you full-force trying to hurt you. Some control is required, so there's a little taken off each technique. However, in street self-defense, if you hold one hand down near the groin, you protect the groin, but you give up protecting the rest of your body. For this reason, it's best to keep the guard up and chamber the legs to protect the groin against kicks, as in Bassai, Pyung Idan, and Pyung Samdan."

The defender (right) moves under the attacker's side kick and unleashes her own side kick to the attacker's exposed groin.

In Bassai, the leg is raised into chamber. The next movement, a hammer fist strike next to the chambered leg, can be interpreted as a strike meant to break the attacking leg near the ankle. In Pyung Samdan, the leg is chambered, protecting the groin, but it's followed with a side kick. "In street self-defense, you open yourself to a groin strike by throwing high kicks," Fox says. "Unless you're very quick with a high kick, and you strike the target squarely and decisively, you're vulnerable."

Consider the necessity of including groin strikes and blocks in traditional Tae Kwon Do forms. Remember—to protect your groin, don't square off to an opponent in class, in competition, or on the street. Chamber a leg against a groin kick instead of giving up guarding your upper body by lowering the hands. In a confrontation, remember that groin strikes work, but you have to strike accurately, powerfully, and quickly.

The Painful Truth

The defender (right) moves under the attacker's high kick with a high block and counters with a groin punch.

Why is a groin shot so incapacitating? "The pelvic area of both men and women holds many nerves, what's referred to as 'complex innervation.' When you take a groin shot, these nerves are stimulated and you experience a very wide range of symptoms," says Dr. Mark Mascari, a Harrisburg, Pennsylvania–based physician and Tae Kwon Do student. "Nerve impulses starting in the groin not only send pain sensation to the brain—they also stimulate the intestinal tract to spasm. This noxious stimulation of the pelvic area's complex innervation can even

slow the heart rate to the point at which the victim may become faint." Furthermore, Mascari says, reflex innervation may cause profuse sweating, and may cause the blood vessels to dilate, dropping the blood pressure and thus also causing faintness.

"Both males and females have the same innervation," Mascari says, "but males may feel more discomfort because of the pendulous nature of their genitalia and the greater shearing forces that can be placed on them. These greater shearing forces cause more traction and stimulation of the nerve endings."

Groin-Shot Treatment

"Most blunt trauma to the groin area can be treated with rest, ice, or cold packs, and in males, scrotal elevation," says Mascari. "In females, vaginal laceration can occur, and quick treatment is required to prevent infection and chronic dysfunction. Anti-inflammatories like acetaminophen, aspirin, or ibuprofen can also be helpful. Any pain in the groin area lasting more than an hour following a strike warrants a consultation with a physician, even with no other symptoms."

Mascari says the following signs should prompt an immediate visit to an emergency room:

- Blood in the urine or the presence of blood at the opening of the urethra.
- Immediate swelling of the scrotum in males, or a laceration of the labia or vagina in women.
- Scrotal pain, or a red or bluish discoloration.
- A red, hot, hard mass at or near the groin that's painful to the touch.

Straight Talk About Groin Cups

A groin cup is the most vital male training item. There are two kinds of groin protectors. Flat, conventional cups are designed primarily for baseball, football, and other sports. They are designed to protect you against a straight-on blow to the front of the body. However, martial artists require the additional protection against strikes rising from below the groin offered by a tuck, or contoured, cup. A tuck cup simply curves slightly more under the body than a flat cup. Groin protectors for boxers, which afford hip and kidney protection, are not tuck-under cups, and they are for the most part too cumbersome for martial arts use.

A cup should fit comfortably and snugly. The supporter, in which the cup is placed, is the key to a proper fit. Supporters are sized according to waist measurement. A properly fitted supporter should hold the cup firmly in place. When your cup starts to move around in the supporter, it's time to buy a new supporter. Supporters loosen through wear and washings. A loose-fitting cup can injure you.

A groin cup is designed to provide vital protection, and in most cases, it does that. Wearing a properly fitted groin cup in training is like wearing a seat belt in an automobile. Wearing one is decidedly prudent, and it's the first step toward lowering your risk of injury, but it is certainly no guarantee against injury. You should also understand a cup's limitations, and exercise appropriate control in training.

Art Michaels is a Harrisburg, Pennsylvania–based freelance writer and Tae Kwon Do black belt. This material originally appeared in the March 1995 issue of Inside Tae Kwon Do *magazine.*

22

Get Hooked on the Hook Kick

Art Michaels

Speed and snap are the keys to developing a powerful, effective hook kick. When properly developed, the hook kick can be used effectively in competition and on the street.

Throwing higher hook kicks stresses the knees. To reduce the chances of injuring your knees, strengthen the muscles and ligaments around the quadriceps, which support the knees. This strengthening is accomplished through weight training and tension kicking.

Tie score. One more point wins. You blink to shake off the exhaustion. You and your opponent gasp for air. He stares at you as sweat drips down his face. You hear the command to fight. You and your opponent cautiously approach each other.

You shuffle. You throw a fast front-leg hook kick that catches your opponent's lead arm, knocking it away to the side. You return quickly with a side kick that lands flush against the opponent's unguarded right rib cage. It's a sure, fast point, and you win! No fancy jumping, no flashy spins, and no high-stepping double kicks here. Your quick hook kick/side kick combination created an opening and you scored. Without that hook kick, though, it wouldn't have happened as quickly or as easily.

"The hook kick can be effective in competition and on the street, but it has to be performed cor-

To execute a rear-leg hook kick from a fighting stance, square up and bring the rear leg up as if you were going into a front snap kick chamber.

Twist your body into a side kick position.

Execute the kick as if you were throwing a side kick. Pivot your hips as you would for executing a side kick or a roundhouse kick.

rectly in order to develop speed and power," says Joe Fox, a Harrisburg, Pennsylvania–based Tae Kwon Do instructor.

Basic Execution

Consider the basic steps in executing this versatile kick. From a fighting stance, square up and bring the rear leg up as if you were going into a front snap kick chamber. Twist your body into a side kick position. Execute the kick as if you were throwing a side kick, but just short of extending the kick and just wide of the target, hook the heel or sole of the foot (either is the weapon) in toward the target. After you've pulled the foot back, reverse the steps to put the foot down. Pivot your hips as you would for executing a side kick or a roundhouse kick. When you throw the hook kick, you also torque the hip at the point of execution, pivoting on your support leg. The hips initially pivot in the opposite direction of the kick, and this gives the kick driving force. As you execute the kick, you rotate the hip—roll the hip to get that pulling-in motion. In this way you don't depend entirely on the knee to do all the work.

"One key to executing this kick properly is that you pull the kick in just short of full extension," Fox says. "You don't want to fire out the side kick part fully and extend the foot completely and then try to hook the kick, because then you'd lose power. Your hook would be only a 'push,' and it wouldn't have the snap, speed, and power that this kick requires." Fox says that the power of this kick comes from the snap at the point of pulling the kick in—like the final snap at the end of a whip.

In a shuffle drill, your partner holds focus pads, and as your partner moves around, you hit the pads with combinations of front-leg, rear-leg, and spinning hook kicks.

Developing Power and Speed

If your target is the head, or anywhere high on the body, you have to be very flexible to execute a hook kick properly. Without flexibility, there's no speed and you just push the kick. If your flexibility is limited, you develop speed and snap by starting low and just getting the form and motion of the hooking and pulling part of this kick.

Throwing higher hook kicks stresses the knees. To reduce the chances of injuring your knees, strengthen the muscles and ligaments around the quadriceps, which support the knees. This strengthening is accomplished through weight training and tension kicking. "Tension kicking is kicking very, very slowly, holding onto your partner or a bar, or just standing and very slowly laying out the kick and pulling it back," Fox says. Another effective strengthening exercise is to hold onto a bar or other support with your foot nearly extended. Your partner supports your foot, and as you slowly hook the kick, your partner offers resistance on the leg. In timed repetitions and sets, this exercise builds strength.

Using shields and focus pads is another way to develop a fast, powerful, and effective hook kick. Shuffle drills with focus pads can help you develop the skill of hitting a moving target. Your partner holds the pads, and as your partner moves around, you hit the pads with combinations of front-leg, rear-leg, and spinning hook kicks. "Shields develop body kicks, but you have to make sure that the person holding the shield lets the shield give a little. Too much resistance against the knee is a lot of shock without some 'give,'" Fox says. He does not recommend throwing hard, powerful hook kicks against a heavy bag because without that "give," performing this kind of drill can stress the knees. Fox prefers air kicks to develop technique, and to increase power and focus he suggests using a kicking shield and focus pads.

Shield work helps you develop body kicks, but you have to make sure that the person holding the shield lets the shield give a little. Too much resistance against the knee is a lot of shock.

"Speed breaks are a way to develop and test a quick, powerful hook kick, especially a spinning hook kick or a jump spinning hook kick," Fox says. "To break a board with someone holding the board lightly between the thumb and index finger, your kicks must have speed and snap. You can't break this way simply by pushing the board, so a speed break is an excellent test to evaluate your technique."

Street Strategies

One effective strengthening exercise is to hold onto a bar or other support, with your foot nearly extended. Your partner supports your foot, and as you slowly hook the kick, your partner offers resistance on the leg.

"If you use a hook kick to strike the body or the legs, the weapon is the heel," Fox says. "Here you'd strike the knee, inner thigh, groin, and solar plexus. To strike the head, extend the foot and catch the target with the bottom part of the heel and sole of the foot as the person leans away from the kick. You get more extension of the kick using the sole of the foot."

You can generate a lot of power with a hook kick to an attacker's hamstring, and you're not throwing a high kick. This kick can cause the hamstring to spasm, or you might even take out the leg completely. If not, the kick can turn an attacker toward you so that you can fire off a kick to the inner thigh or groin, or pursue other combinations. A low spinning hook kick is also an effective sweep. The weapon is the heel. The target is the foot between the heel and the bottom of the calf. This kick's effectiveness comes from the spinning motion, and the speed and torque that spinning generates. A strong hook kick can also let you reach an attacker's groin if the attacker is not squared off to you.

Applications for Competitions

"One way to use a hook kick in competition is to set up another kick," Fox says. "When you use the hook kick to set up another kick, it initially doesn't have a lot of power. You draw the opponent toward the kick for the next, more powerful scoring technique. For example, you could try a hook kick to the back of the opponent's head or body to make the opponent turn around. Then you return with a roundhouse kick to the face or the body."

A hook kick is also useful in bringing down a person's guard. You throw a hook kick to the lead arm, as if you were grabbing the arm with your foot, or knocking the arm out of the way. Come back with a side kick or a front snap kick to the open area of the torso. You can also use a hook kick to wear down a good defender's arms. Repeated hard hook kicks to the arms and shoulders will take their toll.

"If you finish a combination with a hook kick, it should most often be a spinning hook kick," Fox says.

Breaking is a way to develop and test a quick, powerful hook kick, especially a spinning hook kick or a jump-spinning hook kick.

One way to use a hook kick in competition is to set up another kick. Here, Janelle Silvers (right) throws a front-leg hook kick to Todd Bachman's guard, knocking the left hand away.

Silvers quickly rechambers the kick, without dropping the kicking leg, before Bachman can recover, and is prepared to stick a side kick to the open area of Bachman's rib cage.

"A strike to the back of the head is hard to see. The opponent thinks the kick is going wide, and suddenly you hook the kick into the opponent's head for the score." A front-leg hook kick can also make an effective lead technique to go for the score with your first attack. This technique can be effective if you're fast and flexible enough.

These are the kinds of techniques you'd practice with a partner holding focus pads. "The hook kick is actually one of the more advanced kicks," Fox says. "I don't teach it until a student reaches the mid-green belt level. To throw an effective hook kick, you have

to have a decent front snap kick and side kick. If you teach the hook kick too soon, students tend to develop a hooking side kick, which robs that kick of its power. Teaching the hook kick too early also makes it difficult for some students to break the habit of hooking all their kicks."

Conclusion

As you practice hook kicks, remember to build the muscles around the quadriceps, which support the knees. Practice each step in executing the hook kick—don't leave any step out. Work hard with a kicking shield and focus pads. Practice incorporating

You can generate a lot of power with a hook kick to an attacker's hamstring. This kick can cause the hamstring to spasm, or you might even take out the leg completely.

hook kicks into your sparring combinations and self-defense strategies. Remember—low kick or high, snap and speed are the keys to developing a powerfully effective hook kick.

Art Michaels is a Harrisburg, Pennsylvania–based freelance writer and Tae Kwon Do black belt. This material originally appeared in the September 1995 edition of Inside Tae Kwon Do *magazine.*

23

Where There's a Wheel, There's a Way

Tae Kwon Do's Destructive Spinning Wheel Kick

Andrew Breen

The spinning wheel kick is known by a variety of names, including the reverse turning kick and the spinning hook kick. Whatever name one chooses, this kick remains one of the most powerful momentum kicks in the Korean stylist's arsenal.

Few kicks in the martial arts repertoire rival the spinning wheel kick for pure excitement. Practitioners from Korean systems such as Tae Kwon Do, Tang Soo Do, and Hapkido have refined this technique to the point that it is one of their most consistent scoring options for both point and full-contact competition.

In the classic straight-legged version of the wheel kick, the rear leg is swung 180 degrees in a wide arc from its original position toward the intended target—usually the opponent's head. The kicker's torso and supporting foot facilitate this motion with a quick pivot away from the opponent and, much like the revolution of a spinning top, the resulting torque provides impetus to the kicking leg. As the waist begins to rotate, the upper body leans away and the leg moves toward its target. This backward lean serves as a counterbalance and allows for the full

extension of the kicking leg. Despite the name, the straight-legged wheel kick is not initiated with a stiff leg. Instead, the kick is begun with the knee bent in order to increase turning speed. The leg is then straightened at about the halfway point and reaches its target in a locked-out position.

The wheel kick can also be delivered in a looser, quicker fashion by simply turning, bending the knee, and snapping out the lower leg. This variation is somewhat faster than the straight-legged wheel kick; however, it does not deliver the same explosive power. Since it is easier to recover after a miss, the bent-knee wheel kick is frequently seen in point tournaments, where power is not the primary concern. In truth, this version of the wheel kick is more properly a quick turn and then a hook kick. This is not to imply that the kick is not a legitimate technique, merely that it lacks the tremendous centrifugal force generated by the straight-legged wheel kick.

The wheel kick can also be performed with a full turn of the body prior to delivering the technique. Usually used in conjunction with a shallow forward step, the kicker's body completes a 360-degree turn so that the original lead leg becomes the kicking leg. The extra rotation recruits additional momentum and transfers maximum destructive power.

The striking surface of the wheel kick is the back of the heel or, with lesser effect, the sole of the foot. Since the kick is momentum driven and directed at the head, it is a dangerous technique to practice recklessly, especially against a novice dojang mate. Of course, with repeated practice, a practitioner can develop superb accuracy with the spinning wheel kick. Indeed, well-known Tae Kwon Do master Tiger Kim frequently demonstrated his breathtaking mastery of the wheel kick by splattering an apple placed on the end of a sharp knife—a feat he accomplished while blindfolded.

Notwithstanding this degree of extraordinary skill, the average Tae Kwon Do stylist should employ the wheel kick with prudence—both for his own sake and that of his sparring partner. Once unleashed, a committed wheel kick cannot be pulled back or retracted. It can be slowed to minimize accidental contact, but generally, once a practitioner lets it go, all bets are off.

Since the wheel kick is delivered with the rear leg, the extra distance that the foot must travel can provide an opponent with the time to muster a defense. This means that the wheel kick is not the best option for a lead attack—unless a practitioner camouflages the motion with angled footwork.

Angular Approach

By slicing in at an angle, a fighter gains two crucial advantages. First, the distance to the target is decreased without shortchanging the technique.

Instead of chasing an opponent, the kicker intercepts his opponent with the wheel kick. For example, a practitioner in a right-lead stance can either move at a 45-degree angle or, if the opponent is moving forward, he can move laterally at a 90-degree angle. From here the left leg completes its circle and connects with the target before the opponent can adjust to the realignment. The second advantage of this angled approach is deception. When two fighters are squarely lined up, a defender can potentially spot the kick from its conception to its completion. However, if the kicker steps over at a 30- or 40-degree angle, the leg arcs outside the opponent's line of vision. This trajectory effectively eliminates the opponent's peripheral vision as the kick rides in on his blind spot. This deceptive delivery is responsible for the sneaky speed fighters often talk about.

More unsettling than pure miles-per-hour speed, a wheel kick delivered with sneaky speed seems to be there before the defender can react; indeed, an opponent doesn't even see the technique until it is right on top of him—and by then it's too late. A cross-step also allows the kicker to shield the initial phase of the wheel kick with his or her back. Consequently, the opponent faces the double whammy of not seeing the beginning of the kick and not being able to pick up on its altered trajectory, even after it is well underway.

For a linear technique such as the side kick, it is true that the shortest distance between two points is a straight line. Hence, direct lines of attack are appropriate. However, the guiding principle of the wheel kick is the circle, and angled footwork allows a practitioner to exploit the advantages of the circle by dictating to an unprepared foe where it will begin and where it will end.

Timing

Along with utilizing angles efficiently, proper timing is critical to applying the wheel kick. Remember, in the competitive arena, a Tae Kwon Do or Tang Soo Do stylist is likely to be facing off with an opponent who is just as familiar and perhaps just as proficient with the wheel kick. Speed alone is not enough; an opponent's defense must be thrown out of sync—either with a preliminary technique or by using the wheel kick as a counterattack to catch him on the way in.

As part of a combination, the wheel kick flows smoothly from a roundhouse, side kick, or just about any kick that forces the opponent to give ground. A roundhouse or 45-degree kick works particularly well because the follow-through leaves one's body perfectly positioned to turn into the wheel kick. As a counterattack, the wheel kick should ideally be delivered while the opponent is still fully committed to his own attack. Once the opponent has recovered his balance (that is, once the leg has touched down after a kick attempt), it's too late to start your counterattack; the moment is past. Obviously, it is not easy to anticipate the attacks of a competent fighter. Yet this is another instance where angled footwork can make the task easier.

Consider the possibilities that come from employing an oblique angle to evade attacks. You can avoid any linear attack such as a side kick, ax kick, or lunge punch without having to block. Proper footwork takes your body out of the line of attack and frees you up to deliver a counterattack on the same beat. Of course, this tactic is less useful against circular kicks like the roundhouse or the spinning wheel kick. With that provision noted, lateral and oblique footwork enable a fighter to minimize extraneous blocking and launch the wheel kick without getting hit.

In addition to actually scoring on an adversary, the wheel kick inspires respect. Accordingly, it can be utilized to keep an opponent from becoming overly confident with his attacks. Indeed, no one is anxious to be clocked by a full-power wheel kick and the hesitation engendered by this wariness is a potent advantage in and of itself.

Self-Defense Validity

Outside the controlled confines of free sparring, however, the advisability of employing the wheel kick as a self-defense weapon is a matter of some debate. Correctly executed, Tae Kwon Do's wheel kick is capable of transmitting unquestioned knockout force. It doesn't require much imagination to picture the damage inflicted by a fast-moving heel to the jaw or temple. Landing the blow to the face can be similarly devastating, particularly with a direct hit to the nose or mouth. Moreover, the spinning wheel kick is a technique the average assailant is not likely to be on guard against. The same angles used to surprise a sparring partner will be even more startling to an attacker unfamiliar with the motion and trajectory of the wheel kick.

On the other hand, the wheel kick is not without its risks. Even though the kicker's back is turned for only a split second, that may be all it takes for the assailant to move in—with very unpleasant consequences. The momentum from a missed wheel kick also leaves the kicker vulnerable. The wheel kick requires a high degree of coordination and spatial precision, exacting qualities that may be severely inhibited by the tension and total unpredictability of a street confrontation.

In the final analysis, the question of whether the wheel kick is appropriate for self-defense comes down to a personal choice based on each practitioner's individual skill, confidence level, and the circumstances of each situation.

Proper Wheel Kick Training

Timing and execution are developed through tried-and-true methods such as partner training, solo repetitions, and striking drills directed at fixed and hand-held targets. There is no need to devote extensive energy to hitting the heavy bag; in fact, heavy bag work can be counterproductive. The wheel kick derives its power from velocity and proper form, but hitting a heavy, hard-to-move bag can encourage a pushing, tense method of delivery. Conversely, focus mitts or pads are perfect for cultivating speed and accurate placement, both of which are critical to the wheel kick.

It is also a good idea to incorporate stepping, shuffling, and angled footwork into the training done with the focus mitts. A partner will be able to assist this process by moving the mitts into a variety of positions in order to accommodate different angles of impact. If a practitioner does want to make efficient use of angles, partner drills are a good way to reinforce fresh footwork skills. For most martial artists, linear movement—both offensive and defensive—is ingrained. It is not such a simple matter to suddenly change one's movement patterns. Consequently, creative footwork should be integrated into the training as well as into the application of the wheel kick.

There is no doubt about it: mastering the spinning wheel kick demands a heavy investment of effort. It is not a technique that suits every practitioner's tastes or talents—but it is a key element in the Tae Kwon Do arsenal and it is, in fact, part of what gives the kick-oriented Korean systems their unique flavor and excitement. Fortunately, imaginative strategies such as angled footwork can help to make the spinning wheel kick as effective as it is exciting.

Andrew Breen is a Boston, Massachusetts—based black belt and one of the world's finest technical martial arts writers. This material originally appeared in the February 1994 issue of Inside Tae Kwon Do *magazine.*

24

How to Perform Great Demonstrations

Thomas P. Callos

A martial arts demonstration at its best is fun, inspiring, and entertaining. But a poorly organized—or mishap-prone—demonstration can grate on the audience's nerves. You know the kind: the boards don't break, someone forgets his form, a bo-staff flies through a plate-glass window, or a woman knocks out her partner with an accidental, but picture-perfect, kick to the head. Take a lesson from demo-master Ernie Reyes Sr. and his West Coast Demo Team to avoid these and other embarrassing complications.

In search of advice on how to orchestrate a successful and entertaining martial arts demonstration? Who better to ask than the best? Without a doubt, Ernie Reyes's West Coast Demo Team, based in San Jose, California, is the premier martial arts performance troupe in the United States. I polled Reyes and five other original West Coast Demo Team members for performance tips and advice.

Opponent Lee Reyes applies a bear hug to Master Ernie Reyes Sr. Stepping to his left in a low horse stance, Reyes throws both elbows up sharply.

Reyes drives his right elbow into the solar plexus of his attacker. This technique is followed immediately by a right knife-hand to the groin.

Reyes drives another right elbow to the jaw. He steps away and delivers a right side kick to his attacker's midsection.

Ernie Reyes Sr.

"First, be organized; plan, practice, and refine. It's nothing complicated. The best champions and the most exciting performers are usually masters of the basics. Second, make sure your performers are role models—before, during, and after the performance. To teach the martial arts without an emphasis on character diffuses the real power of martial arts, which is the power to create positive change in people's lives. Work and practice together as a team. Every member, like every link of a chain, is equally important. I believe teamwork is the essence of life. How you interact with your life team—like parents, brothers and sisters, teachers, classmates, neighbors, and the audience—affects the quality of your life, theirs, and eventually, the quality of our world."

Margie Betke

"Practice running out to the demo area, turning, and lining up with speed, uniformity, and precision. If you can line up in an interesting way, you've already captured the audience's attention and turned on the electricity. Practice lining up in different formations because you'll have to perform your routines on different-sized stages. Sometimes we would use a basketball-court-sized room to rehearse in, only to find we had to perform in a boxing ring. The way you get out on stage should be polished and professional."

Soo Gin Lee

"Brevity is best when doing demos. Short and sweet. Have an awesome ten minutes that leaves the audience wanting more, instead of a half-hour or longer that leaves them feeling like they've seen it all. Most demos I've watched are just too long and technically redundant. Mesmerize them in the first two minutes, then blow them away in the next eight. For some of our major TV demos, we have to keep everything under three minutes. It's a dazzling three minutes, though."

Scott Coker

"Stick to strong traditional basics. Flawlessly synchronized basics are more impressive than mediocre acrobatics. I think demo teams try to get too fancy. The first *kata* [training exercise set], done flawlessly, is better than jump kicks or fight scenes that are rough and sloppy. Once you have a good basic routine, then build it up and have a dynamic finish."

Gary Nakahama

"Use some humor in your demonstrations. Have some fun when you perform. Part of your performance should be traditional and serious, and part should include something that makes the audience chuckle. A slow motion fight sequence, a giant rubber knife, or a bad guy in a funny costume are all ways you can lighten things up. Playing down the violence with some comedy is especially good for children's audiences. But when using humor in your demos, remember the golden rule: *Don't Overdo It*."

Tony Thompson

"Practice, practice, practice. Pay attention to the little details like hand positioning, head snapping, and stances. Repetition is the mother of skill, and serious, focused practice will give you a first-class team. Practice will cut down on mistakes, accidents, and embarrassing situations. Do your show at slow speed, medium speed, and full-out before you ever get on stage. And remember one of Master Reyes's rules: Don't practice when the audience is watching. Don't give away the show."

Ernie Reyes Jr.

"Cater your performance and music to your audience. An audience of fourth-graders at a school assembly requires a different approach than performing at the Battle of Atlanta. With some demos it might be appropriate to offer narration; at others you just crank up the music and go. Also, be versatile in your demo themes. When demonstrating for school kids, be selective with your techniques. Whatever you do will be duplicated on the playground shortly after your performance. My personal oath is to always give 110 percent in a demonstration, or in anything else that's important to me. My dad taught me to give my heart and soul to each performance, whether for one person, or sixty thousand."

Thomas Callos is a professional writer based in Kailua-Kona, Hawaii. This material originally appeared in the January 1996 edition of Inside Tae Kwon Do *magazine.*

25

The Art of Breaking

John Stewart

Breaking can be a legitimate test of power and focus—or it can be a highly questionable waste of time and energy.

According to Tae Kwon Do breaking expert Gene Biermann, of Horicon, Wisconsin, "The most important aspect of breaking is the confidence it gives a person. I know it sounds a little crazy, but breaking twenty-four two-inch bricks helped me become a better instructor. After doing that break it helped me know more about myself, and it proved to me that my technique was solid. Plus, it gave my students a sense of pride in me."

Many of us have already seen a martial artist crush concrete slabs into cat-box filler. We may have been there when someone decided to bash a brick to bits, or to make eight-ounce tumblers out of sixteen-ounce whiskey bottles by chopping off the tops with his hand. Then, just when we think we've seen everything, someone comes along and converts, say, granite into gravel. Or takes large, round rocks and pounds them into small, jagged pieces. Or caters an affair in which he crushes a stack of ice blocks into party cubes for five thousand.

Breaking is not necessarily difficult, but it can be very dramatic. A large part of breaking any object is making the firm decision that this brick, this board, or this piece of rock is surely going to give way under the force of your most powerful strike. And usually, it does. If the elements of power are all present—speed, focus, and proper form—most martial arts practitioners can break several boards or concrete slabs at once. And when attempted by a highly skilled martial artist—someone with a strong mind and proper conditioning—it is possible to break an astounding array of materials.

The "How" and "Why" of Breaking

Actually, it should come as no great surprise that these things are possible. Human bone has been proven to be many times stronger than wood or concrete, partly because most of the body's bones are filled with a network of tiny cross-bracing struts that provide a resiliency that wood, brick, and concrete do not possess.

High-speed photography has shown that the hand actually flattens out on the object on impact, behaving for an instant as if it were a liquid under the stress of impact. That the hand can survive such deformation, even momentarily, is a tribute to the structure of human bone. And yes, it hurts. Even when the boards or bricks give way as planned, there is likely to be a residual soreness, a long-lasting ache that usually hurts more the next day than immediately upon impact. "When I am doing a demonstration with the crowd out there, I don't have pain," says Hee Il Cho, the well-known Los Angeles–based martial artist. "Afterward, yes, there is pain—of course there is pain. But the pain is in your brain, and it takes patience to endure it afterward. You have to expect that and discipline yourself to take it," he says.

Why is breaking part of the martial arts, and why would anyone want to try it? And if one succeeds in breaking an object, what has been accomplished? It all depends on how one approaches breaking. According to Cho, how you break is more important than what is broken.

"Breaking should be a test of skill, not strength. How many is not important—it's how you do it,"

Cho says. To him, breaking a board should be a test of how powerful a certain realistic, useful technique has become over years of practice. To use a technique that one would not ordinarily use in fighting for breaking is to accomplish nothing, Cho says. For example, to practice and acquire a powerful downward palm strike from a kneeling position—a common breaking technique—does little or nothing for one's perfection of form. That it allows for easy breaking of a stack of boards is therefore irrelevant.

Getting Started

Martial artists should begin breaking with a favorite technique. Cho explains, "If they have a good hook kick, they can test their speed and focus by using it for breaking." And as Cho implies, if they can break boards or bricks with that technique, they can feel fairly confident that they can rely on that technique in a fighting situation. "But getting down on the ground and hitting with the palm—who uses that kind of technique in fighting?"

Cho's attitude is based on his knowledge of the traditional reasons for breaking. The art is said to have been a way of testing power during the birth of karate, when the Japanese occupied the island of Okinawa. The Okinawans of that time, forbidden to possess weapons of any kind, conditioned their hands and feet to an extreme degree of toughness. Since they never knew when they would have to fight against armed assailants, they religiously practiced their technique and tested it against inanimate objects. They had to rely on their ability to land a killing blow in one hard strike, and it was impossible to test the full power of their blows any other way.

Thus breaking, according to some, should be used to test one's favorite and most realistic techniques—a test of confidence, of concentration, and of focus. Today, breaking is sometimes used in testing situations, but more often, it is used in demonstrations. Sometimes these demonstrations are a legitimate performance of fighting techniques, but more often, they are a way for the performer to appear as though he is a consummate martial artist. The temptation is to confuse awesome breaking ability with awesome overall ability. In fact, the great technician can pull off great breaking accomplishments, but the great breaker may not be a good technician overall. The art of breaking is, after all, only a facet of the martial arts. "A martial art is for self-realization," Cho comments. "It's for joining the mind and body, not just breaking. People who only go out and do breaking are like baseball players who only bat or tennis players who can only serve. Yes, breaking is part of the martial arts, but it's not all of it."

And it's not for beginners, even though beginners can be taught to break what would usually be thought of as fairly demanding objects. Cho says he feels the demonstrations he sees today are based on an adolescent fascination with breaking, and that these exhibitions are a disservice to the martial arts. "With those things they show on TV and what they show for demonstrations, the general public doesn't understanding breaking," he says. "These people with hands like girls, breaking with wine glasses or newspapers—that's just fooling the public. How stupid to believe those things. If you don't have the skill, what good is it to trick the public?" he asks. "Let the public realize that breaking shouldn't be a trick. Most of these tricks you see these days, football players or weight lifters could do them better. There should be no reason to cheat."

Techniques and Applications

Cho is equally adamant about the types of techniques he sees in breaking situations. "The breaking techniques they show usually are not used in fighting situations. The measuring, setting up, measuring again—in fighting you can't do that. You have to go—you can't change anything by getting up and down. Breaking is like fighting in that you need speed, balance, and technique. But you can't go out on the street and measure, and remeasure, and then summon your *ki*," he says, allowing himself a small smile.

And then there is the role of the student in the demonstrations—a role that sometimes reveals the extreme degree of loyalty of a student to his instructor. "These demonstrations where they break their helpess fingers—you should never have to make that kind of mistake," says Cho, who feels the public should realize that accidents are inexcusable. "When students get hurt it makes me angry—why should they have to stand there and take the pain? That's no good. I don't think that's right," he says. "Without control, it's really sad."

Cho prefers to demonstrate his own degree of control and power in ways that few other martial artists attempt. He has developed the ability to throw a board into the air and execute a spinning back kick that strikes the board at about head level as it falls. When the heel of his foot makes contact, one half of the board falls down at his feet with the other half sailing off into the distance at high velocity. When Cho breaks, people nearby take cover.

The spinning break is a "speed break," a break accomplished with sheer speed and precision of technique. "You spin right through with speed to do it, keeping the knee bent. To have a straight knee with the spinning kick is wrong; your knee is not going to take it. The knee has to be bent," Cho says. Cho is also fond of demonstrating the power of his spinning back kick by kicking through as many as five tightly held boards, a feat which he sometimes prefers to do blindfolded. To him, the blindfold really doesn't change anything: Cho performs the technique with his eyes closed 90 percent of the time anyway; he knows exactly where the target is, and so he concentrates on his form, rarely bothering to look as he spins through the kick. "There are people who can see through their blindfolds," Cho says. "But for me, there is no reason to cheat."

There are other ways to "cheat" when breaking certain objects. Ice can be scored so that it breaks cleanly and with relative ease. Concrete slabs or blocks can be baked to increase their tendency to crumble. Rocks look hard, but some rocks crumble in the hand. Boards are all different—dry, kiln-baked wood breaks much more easily than green, narrow-grain lumber.

Cho is aware of these ploys—most martial artists are—and he repeats his point about there being no legitimate reason to fool the public. There have been times when Cho has fallen short of his goal of breaking say, six two-inch slabs of concrete laid on top of each other, using the knuckles of his fist. As with any athletic endeavor, sometimes one's energy level is so low that a "best-ever" performance is not possible. Even so, even when the boards or bricks get the better of a person, it need not be a disaster, according to Cho. "Even if it doesn't go through, you don't have to feel bad about it. If you can hit that hard, over and over again, even if you do not break, then they know it [the stack of concrete] is real, and they know something about your spirit. When you can hit hard, over and over without hurting your hand, they know something about your conditioning."

Conditioning

When we asked about hand conditioning, Cho replies that he "builds the calluses during demonstration time. Originally, in the old days, they [the Okinawans] had the calluses, and they could chop through anything. They didn't have contests, so they did breaking. Today we use our hands more for writing and working." He adds, "I don't recommend that students get their hands all crumbled up—you can still train in the martial arts without that. But people who want to be professionals, they may need to. And if you do callus the hand and foot, you can hit harder. It's like the difference between hitting with

a rubber hammer compared to a metal hammer if your hand is conditioned." He says thoughtfully, "If you play piano or are a magician, then you need sensitive hands." But other than people involved in those occupations, most students can afford to undergo some hand conditioning, and Cho mentions specifically toughening the skin on the knuckles by use of a *makiwara* [striking board].

Cho's personal ideas and methods for breaking are contained in his book *The Complete Martial Artist* (Unique Publications, 1981). One of the most sensitive and sincere persons involved in the martial arts, Cho is also a true professional who is capable of genuinely astonishing perfection of technique, particularly with regard to kicking. His trademark kick, the spinning back kick, bursts enough heavy bags that the Everlast people are never surprised to hear from Cho.

Cho's evaluation of the role of breaking in the martial arts is one that many people would do well to consider. Breaking should be a way to test the power and focus of a technique, rather than be an end in itself. To break for the sake of assuming a self-important attitude, or to break with a meaningless technique, is to accomplish nothing of value.

"THIS IS CHILD'S PLAY . . ."

Breaking can be a marvelously spectacular way to make an impression. Unfortunately, sometimes that impression is very strongly negative. The sad truth of this observation was painfully revealed—not once, but twice—to a *karateka* we know whose childlike enthusiasm for breaking far exceeded his understanding of the subject.

"Hey, this is child's play—anyone can break two boards," said our hero at a party. He had just broken two boards, one at a time, at the request of an adoring group of old friends. Enthralled by the attention and accolades, and more than a little addled by several alcoholic drinks, he decided to really make an impression.

"I've got a concrete slab in the car, and if someone will help me bring it up, I can break it for you right here," he said on impulse, giving way to the tempting opportunity to impress his friends. And the prospect of amazing his friends, not to mention the women in the room, filtered through the rosy glow of alcohol, provided an irresistible reason to follow through with his impulsive decision.

He set up the slab, two inches thick, on two coffee cans on the carpet of the apartment. He explained how the power of the hand and mind together would combine to allow him to break the slab. He taped his hand and wrist, mostly for effect, and prepared to hit the slab with a downward palm-heel strike. "I must have beat my hand on that thing for five minutes, but it never did break," he said later. "By the time I was done my hand was all bloody, and actually, I was lucky I didn't break any bones." Was anyone impressed? Not exactly.

Then there was the time our hero, possessed of a sievelike brain that retains learned thoughts only temporarily, decided to break a brick by holding it against a corner of two walls so that the ends rested on two different walls. He quickly attempted a palm strike, but the brick shifted its position during the time it took to cock his hand, falling down slightly. In the following instant our hero ploughed a furrow up his forearm wide enough to plant corn.

Again, this performance did not bring about the intended impressive result. The embarrassment eventually subsided, but our hero had to live with the physical reminders of his foolishness for some time afterward. This brings to mind what breaking is not: breaking is not a vehicle with which to impress friends at a party. It is natural to want to test technique and power as one continues to build

it, but to treat breaking ability as something to be taken out and exhibited, like a new watch one has acquired, is a temptation that ought to be resisted. Even more dangerous, it allows a person to deceive himself.

Since failure provided our hero with a renewed sense of foolishness, perhaps he was punished enough. But if he had succeeded, he now knows, "success" would have only allowed him to continue to pretend that he was something that he was not—to masquerade as a hero that much longer. He learned his lesson, discovering that anyone can break a little bit and that it doesn't really prove anything. Breaking for the wrong reasons can do more damage to a person's ego than it will to his hand.

To break, or not to break? That is the question.
Whether 'tis nobler in the martial arts to endure the slings and arrows of outrageous skeptics;
Or to take the fist against a sea of bricks, and by smashing, end them?
To hit to break—perchance to shatter . . .
'Tis a consummation devoutly to be wished.

(with apologies to William Shakespeare)

This material originally appeared in the November 1981 issue of Inside Kung Fu *magazine.*

PART IV

Self-Defense Principles

26

The Secrets of Olympic-Style Tae Kwon Do Champions

Jane Hallander

According to one trainer of champions, Tae Kwon Do champions are able to fake and deceive opponents; they are experts at trapping movements; they evade strong, powerful techniques from their opponents like a matador against a charging bull, keeping their emphasis on focus, balance, and strength. And they are able to hit designated targets with confidence and a strong will to win. While this sounds like an ad for Superman, it also describes what it takes to be a winner in today's tough Tae Kwon Do tournaments. Here are a winner's secrets.

Now that Tae Kwon Do is an Olympic sport, people are going to want to learn the techniques necessary to win at the Olympic Games and other large Tae Kwon Do competitions.

Although not everyone has had first-hand experience in training Tae Kwon Do champions, Cypress, California–based Pely Ferrer has. He has trained a world champion and numerous national and junior Olympic champions. Among those champions are Dana Martin, six-time national champion and 1993 world champion; Jennifer Grabel Ferrer, eleven-time state champion and two-time national champion; Billy Rabello, national and state champion, and many more. Few people know better than Ferrer what works at Tae Kwon Do tournaments.

Pely Ferrer has been practicing Tae Kwon Do for more than thirty years. As far as developing Olympic

Tae Kwon Do fighting techniques, he believes in hard mental and physical training, with an emphasis on timing. As he says, "Time is gold. Timing is diamond." Here are some of Pely Ferrer's students' winning techniques.

Kicking Techniques

Popular kicking techniques that score points are roundhouse kicks—stationary, advancing, or retreating. Jumping and tornado (jumping and spinning) kicks are also good scoring techniques. Double and triple techniques, such as two or three roundhouse kicks, sliding roundhouses, and skip-jump roundhouse kicks are important parts of a Tae Kwon Do champion's arsenal.

Roundhouse Kicks

There's a good reason roundhouse kicks are so popular. They are one of the easiest kicks to master and one of most powerful. According to Ferrer, if you master only one technique, such as roundhouse kicks, and that is all you have to use, you have a good chance of dominating the fight. Of course, he means all types of roundhouse kicks, not just one. That includes front- and back-leg kicks, as well as the many different kinds of roundhouse techniques. Rapid-fire kicks—such as multiple roundhouse kicks that extend left then right leg, without dropping the feet, in a successive roundhouse kick pattern—are good scoring techniques.

Ax Kicks

Next in importance to roundhouse kicks are ax kicks. Anyone attempting an ax kick must be very flexible to avoid pulling a muscle. He or she must also be fast, able to lift the leg straight up and then hammer downward, hitting with either the heel or bottom of the foot before the opponent realizes what is happening. Good ax kicks require the ability to align the hip correctly for a full leg extension, because the target is the opponent's face.

Spin Kicks

In Tae Kwon Do tournaments, most knockouts come from a spinning hook kick to the opponent's face. If an opponent throws a roundhouse, there is plenty of time to launch a spin kick as the roundhouse comes toward your face. The opponent is already committed to the roundhouse kick and cannot avoid your spin kick.

Ferrer emphasizes that you don't just throw spin kicks whenever you feel like it. Spin kicks are intended to catch opponents off balance as they come toward you. In that situation, you have more power, and they have less balance. A good scoring combination is to start with a roundhouse, followed with a spin kick. The roundhouse sets opponents up by making them react to it. The second spin kick is the one intended to hit and score.

Back Kicks

Back kicks are excellent scoring techniques. Most back kicks are effective either attacking or defending. The target is the center of the opponent's body and face. Back kicks have plenty of speed and power, also serving to remove yourself as a target for the opponent by turning your back to him. Spinning back kicks generate tremendous power as the body mass whirls around toward the target. Timing is important with back kicks. You must be able to spot your opponent for that instant where you cannot see him or her.

Front and Side Kicks

Front kicks are what Ferrer calls "push kicks," literally pushing opponents away. Side kicks are cutting kicks that stop opponents' oncoming kicks, throwing them off balance so you can easily score with another technique of your own. Nowadays many competitors don't use these kicks to score, preferring them as set-up kicks to be followed with a roundhouse, ax, or back kick. However, using either a push or cutting kick to the face is a strong scoring point. A fake cutting kick (side kick) that doesn't completely extend, followed with a jumping back kick, will score well. "It's an advantage for Tae Kwon Do stylists to have a complete arsenal, including techniques such as ax kicks, back kicks, spin kicks, front kicks, and side kicks. While you may dominate the match by mastering one technique, such as roundhouse kicks, you will win more matches if you can deliver more than one technique," explains Ferrer.

Punching Techniques

Punches are not highly scored unless they cause what Tae Kwon Do judges call "trembling shock." The only legal target area is the body's torso on the colored part of the chest protector. Ferrer prefers to have his students use punches as close-range set-ups, tiring opponents and setting them up for scoring kicks. A good example is starting with a punch, then following with an ax kick or roundhouse kick. The punch slightly weakens opponents, enough to make them vulnerable to the kick. The most common punch is the reverse punch.

The Best Techniques for Each Weight Division

There are eight weight divisions in Tae Kwon Do competitions: fin, fly, bantam, feather, light, welter, middle, and heavy. According to Ferrer, those who fall in the fin, fly, or bantam divisions will score well with rapid-fire aerial kicks. Feather and lightweight competitors can also benefit from aerial kicks, although women should use fewer aerial and more combination kicks. Welter, middle, and heavyweight competitors are at their best with roundhouse, back, and ax kicks. Some of these competitors, if very flex-ible, can successfully score with jump spin and back kicks.

Timing

Timing is Ferrer's specialty. The basic principle of good timing is to plan your technique to hit the opponent's head or body and focus on that part of the body. For instance, if you plan to kick the opponent's head, fake low then go for the head—keeping in mind where your scoring technique will hit. If you want to kick the opponent's body, fake a high kick, then kick to the body.

Any time you attempt a technique against an opponent, be aware of what's coming back at you. Remember, when you execute a kick or a punch, you are vulnerable to retaliation.

Jane Hallander is a veteran martial arts writer and a regular contributor to CFW *Enterprises publications. This material originally appeared in the July 1995 issue of* Inside Tae Kwon Do *magazine.*

27

The Counterattacking Revolution
Perception, Technique, and Timing

Master Sang H. Kim

In years past, Tae Kwon Do competition was about who could kick the hardest, and often one kick resulted in a knockout. However, today's competitors have many more weapons available to them. New and faster kicks, exciting footwork, and intricate strategy have changed the face of Tae Kwon Do sparring and brought about the counterattacking revolution. Power alone is no longer the key to winning. Timing, perception, strategy, and the science of counterattacking will determine the sparring champions of the future.

After two grueling rounds of competition, you face off with your opponent in the center of the ring. In just a few minutes, you have learned his moves and he has learned yours. You attack and he evades, he attacks and you block.

Tiring of these fruitless attacks, you both stand watching each other, waiting for the other to make the first move. Losing his patience, your opponent moves in tentatively with a front-leg roundhouse kick and you slide back slightly. As he commits to his attack, you launch a spinning whip kick. Unable to retract his kick, your opponent is a sitting duck. Your kick catches him perfectly and sends him to the mat for the count.

What you just imagined yourself doing is executing a perfect counterattack. One of the most advanced concepts in Tae Kwon Do sparring, coun-

Counterattack I: From an open stance, Carlos Sanchez (left) attacks with a left roundhouse kick; Master Sang H. Kim counters with a right-spinning whip kick.

135

terattacking requires perfect perception, technique, and timing as well as a keen understanding of the mechanics of sparring. Every attack is vulnerable to at least one counterattack. Understanding the intricacies of counterattacking is the key to defeating your opponent every time you step into the ring.

Counterattacking Has the Edge

A competitor who is skilled at counterattacking will always defeat a fighter who is equally skilled in attacking. Why? Consider the above scenario. As soon as your opponent moves to launch his attack, he opens himself for a counter. You on the other hand are still standing in a safe defensive stance. This means that he is attacking a covered target while presenting you with an open target. Clearly you have the advantage. In our example, as your opponent begins to move in for his roundhouse kick, he presents his head as an open target within your kicking range.

Another common example of counterattacking is against a front-leg ax kick. As your opponent moves

toward you with his ax kick, his midsection is exposed and his body is off balance to the rear. A well-timed right-leg back kick to the stomach will send him sprawling backward.

The advantage of counterattacking is that it allows you to avoid your opponent's attack and launch your counter in one movement. By choosing a spinning whip kick or back kick counter, you not only have a perfect scoring opportunity, you can move your body out of your opponent's line of attack in the process. As you turn to kick, you naturally decline your body and all of its vital targets away from your opponent's attack, making it impossible for him to score.

Counterattack III: From an open stance, Sanchez attacks with a left-leg ax kick; Kim counters with an in-place jumping back kick.

The Science of Counterattacking

Counterattacking is not for beginners. Before you study the methods of counterattacking, you must have a firm grasp of Tae Kwon Do's offensive and defensive tactics. Generally, counterattack training is begun after about two years of basic training in sparring methods. To begin developing your counterattacking arsenal, you first have to understand

Counterattack II: From a closed stance, Sanchez (left) attacks with a left-leg ax kick; Kim counters with a front-leg whip kick.

which counterattacks negate each type of commonly used attack. A few examples are:

Attack	Sample Counterattack
Right roundhouse kick	Right roundhouse kick, left roundhouse kick, right punch
Right ax kick	Right roundhouse kick, right whip kick
Right back kick	Right roundhouse kick, double roundhouse kick
Right turn kick	Right roundhouse kick, right ax kick
Right spin whip kick	Right roundhouse kick, right pushing kick
Left pushing kick	Left roundhouse kick, right crescent kick

Counterattack IV: From a closed stance, Sanchez attacks with a right roundhouse kick; Kim counters with a simultaneous left middle block and right punch.

When you begin practicing, start with one of the simple drills above. For example, face your partner in a closed stance (both of you have your left leg forward) and have him or her execute a right-leg roundhouse kick. As the kick approaches, execute your own right-leg roundhouse kick.

This is a simple, in-place drill that allows you to gauge the timing and distance of the kicks. The first few times you may be too slow and get hit by your partner's kick or bang knees. Practice slowly to find the best time to begin your kick. Counterattacking is a technique that emphasizes timing rather than speed—knowing when to move rather than simply moving fast.

Counterattack for a front-leg roundhouse kick. From an open stance . . .

Sanchez attacks with a left front-leg roundhouse kick while Kim simultaneously counters with a right-leg roundhouse kick . . .

followed by a left-leg roundhouse kick ...

and a right-hand punch.

As you progress through each kick and its counterattack, study your partner's movements for openings and consider which kick works best to exploit each opening. Practice timing the kick to take advantage of the opening as it appears. Counterattacking is a precise science. It is not a matter of who is bigger or who is faster, but of who is smarter.

Applying Counterattacks in Sparring

Once you have developed a small repertoire of counterattacks through drill practice, you are ready to apply them in sparring. This is often easier said than

done. In drill practice, your partner cooperates with you. In sparring, you have to time your counterattacks without your partner's help. To speed your progress, limit your sparring practice to the kick you want to develop. For example, agree with your partner that both of you will only use roundhouse kicks for attacking. This gives you both the chance to practice your roundhouse kick counters in a semi-controlled scenario. You know that a roundhouse kick is coming, but you don't know when or with which leg your partner will attack.

When you begin sparring practice, you will discover the variables that enter into counterattacking, including footwork and stance. In competition, your opponent can choose either a left-handed or right-handed stance. This has direct effect on your ability to counterattack. You must develop techniques for each stance. Practice in both left-handed and right-handed stances and with left- and right-handed partners to explore the various possibilities.

Footwork and Counterattacking

Footwork is the next step in counterattacking practice. Executing your counterattack from a standing

Counterattack for a back kick. From an open stance, Sanchez (right) attacks with a right-leg back kick.

Kim slides back and simultaneously counters with a right-leg roundhouse kick . . .

. . . and follows with a double roundhouse kick.

position is fine for drill practice, but impractical in sparring. Your opponent will invariably move toward you to launch an attack. To create enough time to prepare and execute your counterattack, you often have to take a small step or slide, back or laterally. For example, have your partner throw a back-leg roundhouse kick (in an open stance) followed by a back-leg back kick. When he does his roundhouse kick, slide back and slightly to the side to avoid the kick and prepare your back-leg roundhouse kick counter. As he turns for his back kick, begin your roundhouse kick. If you moved correctly, his kick

will pass by you as you score with your roundhouse kick.

In general, always precede your counterattack with footwork to gain the best position for both avoiding your opponent and scoring. When you are very advanced at counterattacking, you may find it more advantageous to stay put and launch your counter. For example, your opponent is rushing in with a back-leg roundhouse kick and you counter with an in-place jumping back kick to his head. While this will certainly shock your opponent, it requires expert technique, timing, balance, and a lot of guts. Standing your ground while your opponent charges in is an excellent way to intimidate him and to establish your superiority in the ring. It is the ultimate in counterattacking.

Fighting a Counterattacker

So if counterattacking is the best strategy in sparring, what do you do when you meet a counterattacker? There are two strategies.

The first is to overwhelm him with a blizzard of hit-and-run attacks. Using confusing footwork, rush in with an attack and then move out quickly or

Counterattack for a side pushing kick. From an open stance, Sanchez (left) attacks with a front-leg side pushing kick.

Kim uses a left-side step and left roundhouse kick . . .

. . . followed by a right-leg inside crescent kick.

clinch, taking away his opportunity for a counter. Never hesitate or feint; pick your chance and commit fully to your attack. Show your opponent your determination to defeat his tactics through speed and strength. This strategy works best if you are a strong, quick offensive competitor.

However, if you are also a counterattacker, the competition becomes a delicate chess match. Each

of you will begin the match waiting for the other to attack. When you realize that your opponent is also a counterattacker, the test of wills begins. Each of you will try to draw the other into attacking first through a series of feints and footwork. Eventually someone will move and the battle is on. You attack, your opponent counters, you recounter and so on. In this type of match, the competitor who can respond the most times comes out the winner— this will be your strategy. Matches between counterattackers are marked by long periods of standing around interspersed with short, intense bursts of furious action as each competitor tries to find the perfect opportunity.

Fighting a counterattacker requires a cool head and patience. Don't allow yourself to get fooled by his feints and false starts. Wait for him to make the first move, but don't fall into a trap. He may give you a deliberate opening as a way of setting you up. Don't be fooled by obvious chances; counterattackers don't have holes in their defense. Instead, distract him with footwork and attack strongly as soon as you see an opening.

Timing for counterattacking. The best timing for a counterattack is when your opponent's foot is at its peak height . . .

. . . or just after your opponent finishes kicking.

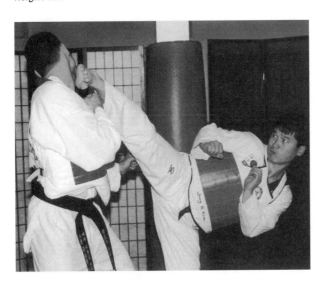

Master Sang H. Kim is the author of Teaching: The Way of The Master, Tae Kwon Do Kyorugi: Olympic-Style Sparring, Ultimate Fitness Through Martial Arts, The Art of Harmony, *and more. He is one of the best-known martial arts seminar presenters and speakers. Master Kim currently teaches at S. K. Tae Kwon Do Academy in Wethersfield, Connecticut. This material originally appeared in the June 1995 issue of* Inside Tae Kwon Do *magazine.*

PART V

Taking It to the Street

28

Tae Kwon Do's Street-Savvy Kicks

Scott Shaw

The debate about the combat effectiveness of Tae Kwon Do kicks has been long and intense. Many, predominantly non–Korean, stylists assert that the Tae Kwon Do kick is much too elaborate to have any effectiveness in street combat. The majority of these critics, however, do not comprehend the actual application of the various Tae Kwon Do kicks or how they were designed to be used effectively.

From a fighting position, your opponent attempts a standard front kick at you, which you block. Follow through with a sliding front kick with the entire weight of your body behind it.

From its origin, dating back many centuries, through its modern redevelopment in the mid-twentieth century, Tae Kwon Do has placed ultimate importance on the legs as appropriate and effective weapons. With this in mind, we can view the individual elements that make up some of the most combat-effective kicking techniques in the Tae Kwon Do arsenal and come to our own conclusion and understanding about the true effectiveness of the Tae Kwon Do kick.

Many individuals initially compare the Tae Kwon Do kick to the use of the hands as a combative weapon. This comparison, in itself, is erroneous, as the hands and the legs are completely different in both their structure and use. The hands, in offensive strategy, may be used in various ways—as a knife-hand, a fist, a backfist, and so on. Though these techniques allow one to be very focused in an attack, none possess the force or power of the kicking techniques that define Tae Kwon Do.

So, why does one use the hands as offensive weapons at all if they do not have as much strength as the legs? As stated, the hands and the legs are two completely different elements of the body, and each must be consciously developed and used according to their strengths and weaknesses to gain ultimate victory in a confrontation. You must develop the effective elements of the hands as well as the effective elements of the legs (which takes much more effort and training) and then link them into one cohesive unit to be a truly effective warrior.

Importance of the Base Leg

To begin our study of the Tae Kwon Do kick, we must first understand the most important thing in the execution of any Tae Kwon Do kick in a confrontational situation. That is to avoid anchoring your base leg (the non-kicking leg) too firmly to the ground. You should always be able to redirect your kicking energies quickly and easily. Assuming that the initial kick is sufficient to defeat your opponent, greatly limits you in any combative situation where, for example, your initial kick is blocked, deflected, or simply misses. You should remain light on your feet, able to either retreat, when necessary, or rapidly change your kicking technique to another form of offense.

From a fighting position, your opponent attempts a straight punch at you, which you deflect with an out-to-in block. Immediately you perform a right inverted roundhouse kick to his head.

This light-footed kicking strategy is developed through continual practice and eventual mastery of the various kicking techniques that are applicable to street combat. Once you achieve this ability, you can quickly redirect or revamp any kicking technique you perform and thus have an even greater ability to win any confrontation.

The Front Kick

To understand the combat-effective Tae Kwon Do kicks, we will start with the most elemental, and debatably the most universally effective, kick in the Tae Kwon Do arsenal, the front kick. The front kick by its very design is fast, penetrating, and effective. However, its effectiveness is limited when it is performed improperly.

The Front Kick's Two Problems

There are two leading problems with the traditional front kick. One is that the novice generally launches it exclusively from the rear leg, and its energy is rapidly expended upward. This gives the traditional front kick very little range unless your opponent remains stationary, directly in front of you. If he simply leans back, out of the front kick's range, the kick will easily miss him. Thus, when applied in this manner, the front kick becomes largely ineffective. The second flaw with the traditional front kick is that it can be easily countered by the trained opponent who quickly rushes in on it, leaving the kicking technician off balance and prone to a counterattack.

What, then, can be done to make the front kick truly effective? There are two variations of the traditional front kick that not only add to its power but greatly diminish your opponent's ability to deflect it.

First, instead of launching the front kick from the rear leg in the traditional way—with the kick's energy rapidly expended in its movement upward so that the kick may fall short of its target—you should launch it from the rear leg in a manner that allows the momentum of the kick itself to propel the entire weight of your body into the target. This is accomplished by allowing the foot of the base leg to slide lightly along the ground until you are close to your opponent. Once the kick's impact is assured, then and only then is the bottom part of the kicking leg snapped out at your opponent and impact actually made.

From a fighting position, by rapidly stepping in at your opponent, you perform a stepping crescent kick, while you check his attacking arm in place.

This form of the front kick is not necessarily targeted at high levels on your opponent's body, such as under his jaw, though it certainly can be. It may, however, be more effectively directed to his midsection, which is a larger target area. By performing the front kick in this fashion, not only do you add range to the kick, but you avoid the common mistake kicking novices make of wasting the kick's momentum.

The second procedure for making the standard front kick effective is to launch it from a front-leg position when your opponent is charging in at you. When you perform the kick at such a time, you can easily target your adversary under his jaw, in his groin, and so on. The momentum he has developed will make it difficult to redirect his assault to avoid your kicking technique.

The Inverted Roundhouse Kick

Little-known yet similar to the front kick is the inverted roundhouse kick, also known as the inside front kick. This kick is performed by bringing your kicking leg slightly in across your body as it is rapidly brought up into its final target, which is generally the head or under the arm of your opponent. This kick is snapped up at knee level, similar to the front

kick, but instead of moving straight up it crosses your body diagonally. Thus, a right-leg inverted roundhouse kick would allow you to powerfully impact the right side of your opponent's head.

As an offensive tool, the inverted roundhouse kick is ideally suited to follow a defensive block. For example, once your opponent's oncoming punch has been deflected, or his punching arm is locked, you can easily strike him with this kick. This effectiveness comes from the close proximity to your opponent because once his punch has been blocked at this range, you can easily grab his arm or a piece of clothing and lock him into place long enough to effectively perform the kick.

The Crescent Kick

The crescent kick, another linear offensive weapon in the Tae Kwon Do arsenal, is sometimes referred to as an ax kick due to the fact that it is brought straight up and its impact, generally to the opponent's shoulder, comes forcefully down with the heel of your kicking leg. This kick is extremely effective in close-quarter fighting since you can grab your opponent by his clothing, thus halting his movement for an instant and allowing you time to powerfully

You face off with your opponent. Instantly you deliver a stepping side kick to his body, penetrating all of his defenses.

lift your leg and forcefully slam it into his shoulder. The crescent kick, along with the inverted round-house kick should eliminate the misconception that Tae Kwon Do's kicks are ineffective in tight fighting situations.

As a defensive technique the crescent kick can have a devastating effect. For example, if your opponent launches a punch you can deflect it with an in-to-out block by immediately bringing the crescent kick up and striking your opponent with it. The crescent kick is equally effective as a rapid and penetrating lead-in technique when it is used in stepping or skipping fashion. To perform the kick this way, your base leg rapidly steps behind your kicking leg as you quickly move in toward your opponent. The kicking leg is brought up simultaneously, on the vertical, until you achieve appropriate kicking distance. Then you unleash the power of this kick onto your opponent's shoulder.

Not only is the stepping/skipping crescent one of the most powerful kicks in the Tae Kwon Do arsenal, it is very difficult to defend against due to the speed with which it is performed. Your opponent only has one option to evade this kick, and that is to get out of the way. You can easily keep your opponent from escaping the kick by grabbing onto a piece of his clothing as you rapidly move in, thus holding him in place as you perform the kick.

The Side Kick

The standard side kick, practiced so often at Tae Kwon Do dojangs around the world, can move from the realm of a relatively ineffective kick to that of strategic weapon in combat when its execution is just slightly altered. Like the basic front kick, the traditional side kick launched from the rear leg has limited range. However, if you simply avoid anchoring your base leg too firmly to the ground, as is generally the case with the traditional version of the side kick, you allow your base leg to be propelled or slid

Your opponent moves in at you and you halt his movement with a side kick.

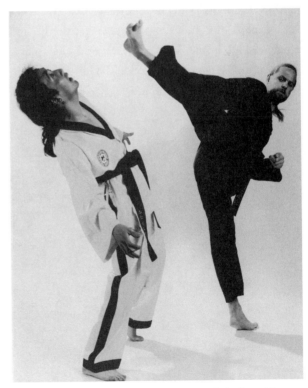

You follow through with an additional side kick to his head.

slightly forward across the floor, following the momentum of the rear leg as it launches into the kick. This not only adds enormous range to the kick, but increases its power as well by putting the force of your entire body behind it. Furthermore, by allowing your base leg to be less rigid, you add an enormous amount of speed to this basic kick.

The front-leg side kick is not only a very rapid means of self-defense, but it will stop the oncoming opponent in his tracks quite effectively. Your opponent rushes in at you with an aggressive technique. By side-kicking him from your forward leg, aiming at his rib region, you will generally go underneath his offensive technique. And you will initially hold him at bay in order that you may continue through and perhaps launch a second side kick at his head, or another counter-defensive technique, to achieve victory.

Again, we see that by simply allowing ourselves to become light on our feet, we can make the most standard of Tae Kwon Do kicks quite useful, dispelling all doubts as to their ultimate effectiveness.

Perhaps the most individually powerful and effective kick in the Tae Kwon Do combat arsenal is the stepping or skipping side kick. This kick is performed by allowing the base leg to rapidly move behind the kicking leg (as with the stepping crescent kick), thus giving you added distance. Then the kicking leg is extended in side kick fashion to impact your opponent. The stepping side kick rapidly penetrates your opponent's zone of defense. And by its very design, this kick has the potential to injure anything it hits. Not only effective in tournament fighting, on the streets the stepping side kick can instantly end a confrontation.

The stepping side kick is not only rapid and powerful but defense against it is quite difficult due to its speed. Your opponent's only option may be to rapidly retreat from its onset, in which case you simply continue through with an additional rapid step behind your kicking leg to give you more distance, and then unleash the kick. Alternatively, your opponent may move to one side of the kick. If this occurs, a backfist or straight punch technique can be launched instantly, depending on which side of your body your opponent has side-stepped to.

The Back Kick

A similar technique to the side kick, structurally speaking, is the back kick. The back kick, generally

From a fighting position, your opponent attempts to front kick you and you block it. Follow up with continual back kicks . . .

. . . finishing him off with a jumping back kick.

misunderstood, is one of the most effective kicks in the Tae Kwon Do arsenal, as has been demonstrated in numerous tournaments. The back kick is executed by pivoting your body behind itself on the ball of the foot of your base leg, and using your kicking leg in a spinning side kick fashion.

This kick not only leaves very few vulnerable strike points exposed to your opponent, but can be used in a continual sequence from one back kick on to the next, and even the next, if desired. The problem that many practitioners have with the back kick is based on the fact that they are performing it incorrectly. First of all, your head must always pivot first to locate your target before the kick is ever launched. In this way, if your opponent moves, you can simply choose a different offensive technique.

In addition, the back kick is not limited to the range that your kicking leg can achieve from its base position. The back kick should be launched deeply into your opponent. This is accomplished by allowing the momentum of the kick itself to extend the entire weight of your body deeply into your target—similar to the distance technique applied to the front and side kick discussed earlier.

The common defense against the back kick is to step to the side or step back. If your opponent steps

to the side, the motion of the back kick can continue into that of a spinning heel kick, which is, of course, much more elaborate, yet nonetheless may be very effective in this situation. If your opponent retreats backward, the rapid execution of one extended back kick followed by another will eventually target him. Furthermore, the impact of the first back kick may send your opponent back again. Continuing through with additional back kicks will no doubt assure your victory in the confrontation.

As we have seen, once the nuances of the Tae Kwon Do kicks are truly understood, not only are they very effective in tournament competition, but they may be put to use victoriously in street combat. Those who criticize them lack either the desire or the ability to practice these combat techniques and put them into proper use.

Scott Shaw is a Hermosa Beach, California, writer, actor, and filmmaker and a veteran Hapkido black belt. This material originally appeared in the April 1994 issue of Inside Tae Kwon Do *magazine.*

29

Nine Strategies to Enhance Your Self-Defense Training

Bill Feltt

Most martial artists—Tae Kwon Doists included—practice self-defense dressed in traditional attire and in the dojang under ideal conditions, far from the reality of the street. But to never train under conditions similar to the street is like preparing for jungle warfare by holding war games in the barracks. Clothing, lighting, environment, and state of mind all play a role. Here's how to train for the street—before the "bad guy" gets in your face for real.

Most Tae Kwon Doists, like other martial artists, train in well-lit, comfortable surroundings while dressed in traditional uniforms. But how often do attacks occur under ideal conditions? Never. No doubt you will be attacked in a less kick-friendly environment—at night on a dark street corner, in some dismal area suited to the nefarious intentions of some thug, or even in the relative safety of your home. So Tae Kwon Doists would be wise to venture out, at least once in a while, to train in alternative settings to enhance their self-defense skills. This should include training in different environments, under low light, and in clothing other than the traditional *dobok* (practice uniform).

After Dark

Darkness changes everything. Shadows are longer, people look different, their appearance and intentions shrouded by the cover of night. Darkness allows muggers to hide in places that daylight would not allow. And, although the best self-defense advice is to stick to well-lit routes, journeying into the darkness may be unavoidable. So the most Tae Kwon Doists can do is to practice in darkness, which may be logistically difficult for many schools. But there are ways to at least approximate poorly lit conditions. Training at early evening with the lights off is one way. Dimming the lights is another.

The object of low-light training should be twofold: one, to heighten sensitivity to movements in the periphery, which increases vigilance to surprise attacks; and two, to get used to punching, kicking, or throwing in low-light conditions. This is easy enough in line drills, but at some point you'll need to practice sparring of some kind in low light, also—possibly a dangerous undertaking, for obvious reasons. Sparring in total darkness is not recommended. Sparring in low light tends to throw off your balance. Moving around in the dark can cause disorientation and a feeling of falling. Also, darkness muddles depth-of-field perception. So sparring in low light requires cautionary measures. Students should suit up in heavy protective equipment. Fortunately, to increase the comfort level in darkness, there are alternative drills to one-on-one combat.

But any form will do. Practicing blindfolded or even in the dark will help heighten your senses and prepare you for low-light confrontations.

Is Someone There?

Sensitivity training helps to heighten your awareness of a "presence"—but not of his intentions. (It's interesting to note that women do much better at this than men.) Students stand in a circle around a blindfolded student, or the subject can simply shut his or her eyes. One at a time, students approach the subject from different angles. As the subject senses a presence, he or she points in the direction of the approaching student. This drill teaches students to be aware of subtle ambient changes. Air movement, sounds, faint changes in lighting, and that inexplicable "sense" of another's presence tip off the observant student to impending danger. There's nothing mystical about this kind of training. It simply forces students to pay closer attention to their senses, stretching their awareness and observation skills to their fullest potential.

Blindfolded forms. Forms can provide an opportunity to practice techniques under low-light conditions, especially complicated forms and forms that require you to keep your balance.

Good Form

While some martial artists may criticize form training, doing forms while blindfolded or with the eyes shut will develop low-light coordination. This can

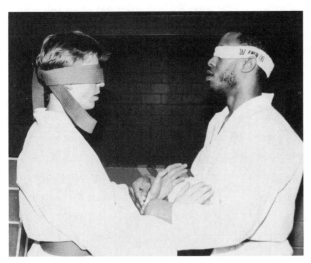

Practicing sticking hands blindfolded will help you rely more on feel than on sight to defend yourself should the fight move in close.

help quell some of the disorientation that may occur in the dark. The more complicated the form, the more difficult it will be to stick to the set pattern and the more effective the exercise. This sounds easy, but a few tries will soon demonstrate otherwise.

Sticky Situations

"Sticking hands," popularized by Bruce Lee, will help the student get a feel for grappling in the dark when practiced in low-light or while blindfolded. To do this, face off with another student, make contact at the wrist and forearm area, and try to maintain contact while your partner moves his or her arms in semicircles, attempting to break contact. Or, modify the drill by trying to break through and grab the lapels.

Dress for Success

How often do you don your dobok for a night on the town? In bare feet? Doing techniques while wearing street clothing can further simulate street conditions

and enhance the reality of your self-defense training. You should try this with clothing you normally wear. Jeans differ from slacks in the way they affect technique. If you normally wear slacks you would be wise to practice in slacks. You'll soon see that street clothes will at the least hamper kicking, perhaps rendering high kicks ineffectual. Tight-fitting jeans will make any kick above the knee impossible, or at least risky. Tight clothing in general will make defending yourself more difficult should the need arise.

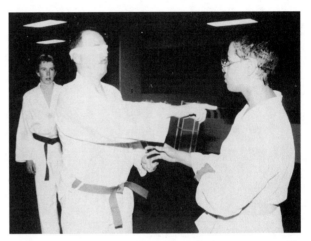

Sensitivity training adds a whole new dimension to martial arts training. A blindfolded student stands at the hub of the circle of students. As quietly as possible, students approach one at a time. The blindfolded student points to the others when he or she senses their presence.

Shoes make kicking interesting, to say the least. Depending on shoe type and surface texture, shoes could increase traction above what you're used to, thus slowing down pivoting for some kicks. Or they could decrease traction, thus making pivoting a slippery experience. Either way, shoes force you to change the way you kick and the way you move. It would be wise to practice techniques with tennis shoes and hard-soled shoes, to avoid falling flat on your back when push comes to shove.

Training in street clothes also provides a reality check for your techniques. The loose fitting and often crisp traditional martial arts garb may snap and pop with punches or kicks. All that noise may not be a true indication of power. Sweats or other common clothing will not react the same and may seem to limit your power, consequently lowering your confidence level. In addition, the weight of the shoes also factors into your kicking power, speed, and ultimate effectiveness.

Practice in the Park

Parks make ideal areas for practicing self-defense outside. Grass not only provides a realistic setting, but also makes a great mat to cushion break falls. Cement or pavement should also be used as training sites, for footing practice only. Obviously, throwing techniques aren't recommended on these surfaces. Training in the park at dusk or dawn provides a realistic backdrop. Make an effort to find a good place away from prying eyes; a group of people practicing martial arts techniques seems to draw onlookers of questionable character.

Down but Not Out

Attacks can occur at the most awkward moments in the most awkward of positions, not necessarily while you're strolling down the street. Training from a sitting or lying position helps prepare for those circumstances. Defending from either position creates a different set of problems. Both make movement awkward, rendering you vulnerable to attack while limiting counters. Practicing from these positions, with some guidance, will help you discover some "tricks" that will prepare you.

Crowd Control

Although most attackers, depending on their motives, want to isolate their victims from others, attacks can occur while others are around. Sometimes this happens in bars or on a busy sidewalk. So it can be helpful to practice self-defense as non-participating students stand around nearby, as if on a dance floor or a crowded street corner. Kicks and punches would have to be modified in this situation to avoid striking innocent bystanders. Better yet, use short punches, knee strikes, wrist locks, or grappling techniques in these encounters.

Drive Safely

Because carjacking is now a popular scheme of car thieves, training behind the wheel is also worthwhile. You can be highly vulnerable in a car, especially while wearing a seatbelt, which protects you in a crash but restricts your movement in the event of an attack. The seatbelt could also prevent you from being dragged from your car. An attacker typically enters the car and hides in the back seat or approaches you while you're stopped at a traffic signal.

A few commonsense tips will help to avoid these extravehicular hazards in the first place, before you're forced to fight your way out of a four-way stop or out of the parking lot at work. Keep the doors locked and the windows up, while driving or when parked. Because keeping your windows up while driving may not always be practical, awareness training can prepare you to react to someone approaching you from the periphery. And always check the back seat before you open the door.

Keep It Real

Many environments can be used as backdrops for self-defense training. Some will enable you to use your style of self-defense, while others will force you to adapt to the environment. So remember, creating a realistic context—in lighting, location, clothing, and any other elements—for your self-defense training will greatly enhance your chances of succeeding should you face an attacker under less-than-ideal conditions.

Bill Feltt is a Springflield, Illinois–based Tae Kwon Doist and freelance writer. This material originally appeared in the August 1995 issue of Inside Tae Kwon Do *magazine.*

30

Fourteen Streetwise
Tae Kwon Do Tips

Jane Hallander

Tae Kwon Do street self-defense techniques include far more than the kicking arsenal for which this art is generally known. Here are fourteen "commandments" used by one northern California instructor.

Throughout history, Tae Kwon Do has been a powerful means of self-defense, emphasizing empty-hand combat. Tae Kwon Do originated as a defensive martial art designed to be destructive to the opponent. In days of old, a punch to the face wasn't an illegal technique, as it is now in Tae Kwon Do tournaments.

Tae Kwon Do stylists originally used their elbows and knees, low kicks, throws, and jointlocks along with the high kicks the art is known for today. Since at that time it wasn't a sport, all kinds of fighting techniques were included in its arsenal. Tae Kwon Do was used to condition fighters for life-and-death battles, not competition. Nowadays, sport Tae Kwon Do is perhaps the martial art closest to the reality of combat, with safety—there is strong physical contact with limited destructive techniques.

Tae Kwon Do is still a powerful self-defense art. Cypress, California instructor Pely Ferrer teaches both the sport and self-defense aspect of Tae Kwon Do. "Tae Kwon Do doesn't have to be all kicking techniques on the street," he says. "The kicking techniques are emphasized in traditional Tae Kwon Do because the leg is a longer natural weapon and is strong and powerful. On the street, if a situation doesn't warrant a kick, there's no reason to have to use a kick. Those who think that studying Tae Kwon Do means you have to use only kicks are wrong. Throughout basic training we execute basic blocks and punches, ridge-hands, knife-hands, palms, elbows, knees, head butting, grabbing, and even eye gouges," explains Ferrer.

In fact, some of Ferrer's favorite Tae Kwon Do defensive techniques are practical elbow strikes, jointlocks, and even head butts. The head butt, for instance, works well as a defense against a bear hug. Elbow strikes often follow knee strikes, taking advantage of a doubled-over opponent. Short leg sweeps lead to takedowns, where finishing blows are often elbow strikes to the head. Kicking techniques, when used, are usually low—aimed below the waist. When self-defense means the difference between life and death, anything goes. Traditional Tae Kwon Do taught everything along with discipline and the right attitude to make the techniques work.

Streetwise Techniques

Ferrer teaches fourteen "commandments" of freestyle sparring to sport Tae Kwon Do competitors. While the focus was originally on tournament contests, many of the commandments are useful in street-fighting situations. Ferrer's commandments are as follows:

1. If you are scared, the chances are good that your opponent is also scared. In a situation where you and your opponent do not know each other, you probably appear just as frightening to your opponent as he does to you. Maintain a calm expression and do not show your fear.

2. Good concentration comes from meditation, scientific training, and physical conditioning. If you are prepared physically and mentally for the fight, there should be little to distract you.

3. You should develop your own individual style and specialize in one technique that you can always rely on in a pinch. A simple, effective technique will get you out of more tight spots than something you have seen someone else do and you have not practiced enough. Different techniques work well for different individuals.

4. At the beginning of the fight, you should take the initiative and try to end the fight with a finishing technique. If you are unsuccessful at seizing the initiative, be on your guard, maintaining a strong defense. Be ready to take advantage of openings as they develop. If you fall behind, you must again try to take the initiative, since you have nothing to lose. Never give up. When both people are tired, the fighter with the most determination has the greatest chance of winning.

5. Check your opponent's stance for weaknesses and adjust your stance accordingly to counter it. You must be aware of your opponent at all times and act accordingly.

6. Change your stance often to confuse your opponent. Secure your balance and relax your muscles. Maintaining the same stance makes you predictable and limits the techniques you can execute. Different stances use different muscles. Muscles fatigue easier if not given a chance to rest.

7. Follow through with each technique. Don't do anything halfheartedly. Anything done

without conviction is wasted effort. Always deliver 100 percent of your spirit and power.

8. Conserve energy, especially in a street fight where you may have to fight several individuals within a short time.

9. Take aim objectively and pick out targets carefully. However, do not look where you intend to strike your opponent or he will know what to expect.

10. Use your entire body in every movement; never punch with just your arm or kick with just your leg. Whole-body movement is more efficient, giving much more power to your techniques.

11. Use your blocking hand as a lead when counterattacking and follow with a strong punch or kick. This adds speed and surprise to your counterattacks.

12. Keep an efficient, light, but still strong guard at all times. One hand should protect the face, while the other protects the solar plexus and below. Feet should always be at least shoulders' width apart.

13. Try to maintain eye contact with your opponent. It is easier to anticipate your opponent's techniques if you watch his eyes. Ferrer explains that there are different schools of thought about eye contact. Some say you should look into the eyes. Others say look at a triangle made of the points of the opponent's chin and both shoulders. Still others say to look past the opponent to utilize peripheral vision. Ferrer believes the best way is whatever works best for each individual.

14. Use a loud *kihap* (yell). Do not drag it out. A good, sharp *kihap* shows fighting spirit and helps your breathing, but drawing it out uses much needed oxygen.

Conclusion

Tae Kwon Do street self-defense also includes techniques against multiple attacks, such as grabbing, holding, and throwing techniques. Ferrer maintains that a well-trained Tae Kwon Do fighter is able to protect against more than one attacker. He or she tries to eliminate opponents as quickly as possible by perfecting vital attack points, such as pressure-point strikes.

Anyone can get hurt or knocked out in a street fight, even the best-trained martial artist. However, martial artists are trained to expect the unexpected. They should know to react with complete awareness and speed. Awareness, of course, includes avoiding fights by controlling oneself or just getting away from a bad situation before it turns violent.

Jane Hallander is a veteran martial arts writer and a regular contributor to CFW *Enterprises publications. This material originally appeared in the January 1996 edition of* Inside Tae Kwon Do *magazine.*

PART VI

Beyond the Technical

31

Fine-Tuning the Student-Instructor Relationship

Diane Reeve

There is no more important relationship in the martial arts than that of the student and instructor. But making that relationship effective for both takes a great deal of work. Each has his or her own responsibilities; if these responsibilities are not well understood, then both people lose. Here's an uncompromising look at the multifaceted aspects of the instructor/student relationship from both perspectives—so each will know what to expect from the other.

The Instructor's Responsibilities

To Teach

The first responsibility of the instructor is to impart knowledge to the student. That's why the student is there in the first place, to learn. Further, the instructor is obligated to teach in a certain fashion, based on the needs of the student. If the student is a child, for example, the teaching must be more concrete and more organized, each step building on the previous step. If the student is an adult, however, a whole different approach should be taken. Adults learn best on a "need to know" basis. Thus, knowing why the adult student wants to learn martial arts becomes paramount in how the student is approached.

In addition, personalities play a big part in how students are taught. As I came up through the mar-

tial arts ranks, I found it curious and somewhat disturbing that my instructor called on me to spar with only women and children during class. I felt a little frustrated because I believed that I would never get any good fighting experience until I was able to spar bigger folks, like the adult men, and those with more experience. So I asked to stay after class and spar eight or ten extra matches just to get good experience. Later, I respectfully questioned my instructor about why he never let me spar the guys in class. Unfortunately, I learned that it wasn't because he thought I'd hurt them! He told me he had looked at the situation from the perspective that if it had been his own wife out there whom he'd called up to spar with a big brown or black belt, she would have just folded right then and there! And that's where personality comes in. Mine was such that I needed that extra challenge to help me improve. His perception was that if he put me in that situation, he would lose me. (By the way, after that I noted that he let several of the women spar the men in class.)

To Guide

In Japanese, the instructor is known as *sensei*, which, literally translated, means "the one who goes before." With the rank comes the responsibility, and in this case, the responsibility is to guide the student. Certainly no martial arts training is without its bumps and bruises, both physical and mental. Through the path to black belt and beyond, the student needs a sensei to guide or direct him or her through the pitfalls of martial arts training.

How do you deal with the boredom that sets in with practicing front snap kicks and backfists a thousand times? What about the frustration that hits when the brown belt plateau sets in? How about dealing with belt exam anxiety? And who hasn't wondered how to deal with pondering, "Am I really good enough for the next belt level?" All these pitfalls may be addressed by a kind, caring, and patient sensei to guide the student along the way. Having someone who's there for him or her, who's actually been through exactly the same thing before, is comforting and immensely helpful to the student. If handled correctly, it can mean the difference between whether or not a student continues in martial arts or becomes one of the multitude of martial arts dropouts. If we as instructors believe that martial arts are good for people—and we must, or we shouldn't be teaching—then we must be there to guide our students though these personal trials and tribulations. It's crucial for them, and it's part of our responsibility, too.

Guidance may also, for some students and instructors, come in the form of personal advice. Some instructors see their role as one to provide wisdom regarding personal issues in their students' lives. This can include everything from job to marital to child-rearing difficulties. If the student seeks

counsel, some instructors will feel obligated to intervene. To me, this is a personal preference based on life experience and qualifications, as well as whether the instructor is teaching at a commercial or traditional *dojo* (training hall). Some traditional instructors feel it is a duty to assist students in coping with life situations. Others wouldn't touch it with a ten-foot pole. I'm in the middle of the road on this one. If it's something I feel comfortable advising on—something I've had experience with or feel qualified to answer—typically, I'll try to help. With a nursing degree as well as two kids, lots of times I'm able to help students through certain issues. But if it's something with which I'm totally unfamiliar, I'd just as soon pass. I'd rather refer to another source or be honest and tell a student "I don't know" rather than give the wrong advice. I think most instructors feel this way. If it's a traditional dojo, the instructor probably can afford a closer relationship and will therefore be more willing to risk giving advice. Commercial school instructors may not be willing or able to take that risk.

To Lead by Example

Since they're in the business of giving advice, instructors have to lead by example. What respect would anyone have for a minister or priest whose ethics were not up to par? By the same token, then, an instructor who preaches to students to keep training but doesn't make the effort to stay "tuned up" himself is not going to have students paying attention for long. An instructor who advises students to stay calm if a sparring partner gets a little out of hand yet comes back viciously when the same thing happens to her is not leading by example. This is especially true for children. The old maxim "Do as I say, not as I do" doesn't work in the dojo. All students learn by example.

I don't know how many times I've complimented one of my black belts on how hard he trains and how dedicated he is to improving. Without fail, he always comes back with, "It's just because you've been such an inspiration to me with your own training." That's the kind of example that makes both instructor and student feel good.

To Critique Without Criticism

Here's where most instructors fall down on the job. Sometimes it comes from a lack of experience (age), or just a lack of maturity (ego), but it can really make or break a relationship. When my brown belts begin to teach, I start to impart this concept to them. Usually, I'll ask a question: "Is it more important to point out everything that a student is doing wrong all at once, or best to just give that student one or two things to work on at a time?" Of course, if you try to tell students everything they are doing wrong all at once, they will just get overwhelmed and frustrated and want to quit.

This was particularly hard for one of my black belts, Max, to understand. At thirteen, he was very intelligent and extremely quick to pick up on things. I taught Max somewhat differently than I taught my other students because he was able to absorb and put information to use so much faster than the "normal" students. But, as he learned, not everyone—in fact, hardly anyone—can be taught that way. When Max was asked the above question, he responded that he felt it was his responsibility as an instructor to point out everything a student was doing wrong. Well, yes and no. Yes, eventually, students should know how they can improve in all different areas. But no, certainly not all at once. When this was pointed out to Max, I think he began to understand how unique and special he really was.

Then, too, how the information comes across is very important. If the tone is angry, disgusted, or belittling in any way, the very heart of what matters in martial arts—building self-esteem—is destroyed. Criticism has to be put in very positive terms. First compliment, then state what is needed in positive terms. Instead of saying "Don't look down," say

"Look at your imaginary opponent." Instead of saying "Don't drop your hands" say, "Keep your hands up." Then, reassure students that you have confidence in their ability to meet the expectation by saying, for example, "That's right," "Good," and so on. This is an excellent way to build skills without destroying egos in the process—a delicate balance for sure, but something for which the instructor must take responsibility.

To Promote Growth

Like with Max, my teenage black belt, and the brown-belt students I ask questions of in class, promoting growth in positive life skills is a vital aspect of the instructor/student relationship. In other words, as sensei, my obligation is not only to teach Tae Kwon Do, but to teach my students how to teach. That involves bringing them to a point ego and maturity-wise that they can make a positive contribution to another life. And it involves watching carefully to assure that no "fatalities" occur. I don't mean physically, but just as important, psychologically. It's helping them learn how to identify needs, use constructive criticism, and build instead of destroy.

But that's teaching the teacher—a level up from where we start. Where we, as instructors, start, is to identify needs and weaknesses in students and begin to establish a base of support from which they are able to build and grow. For example, a female student may come to you with a history of abuse or assault. Therefore, building confidence in herself and releasing some of her anger is going to be a prime factor in helping her grow. A ten-year-old comes to you with ADD (Attention Deficit Disorder)—lots do, by the way—and your prime goal becomes to help this child learn focus and discipline.

An instructor's job is not to teach someone how to kick and punch, though that's certainly a big part of what instructors do. A sensei has a larger responsibility to help the student become all he or she can be. Every child won't be a first-place forms competitor, every black belt won't make the Olympic Tae Kwon Do team, but each and every one can become a better human being as well as a better martial artist. And that's where the student's responsibilities come in.

The Student's Responsibilities

To Train

First and foremost, a student's responsibility is to train. Students who don't practice will never progress past the most elementary level. Part of the growth process that occurs in martial arts is just the plain old everyday hard work that goes with doing something over and over and over again until one gets really good at it. Someone once told me that it takes three thousand repetitions before an action becomes automatic. Students must be willing to go through the effort and sweat it takes to make their motions automatic, clean, smooth, and fast. This causes a metamorphosis, in that the physical action of repeating motions generates the psychological changes common to accomplished martial artists—focus and discipline, to name two. And along with the improved performance that comes with diligent practice comes self-esteem. So training generates quite a few positive life skills in and of itself.

To Think

Not all of martial arts is physical, however. A big part is mental. The student's responsibility (outside of class) is to think about what has occurred in class. This encompasses everything from an analysis of motion to figuring out new techniques to try in sparring. One of my instructors once told me he expected his students to practice five hours outside of class for every one hour in class. Part of that, of course, is physical practice. But part of it, too, is mental. Students should use creative visualization to mentally practice their ideal performance on the mat.

A study was once done to test the theory that visualization improves performance. Martial artists were divided into three groups: one group did nothing differently, the second group focused on pleasant thoughts, and the experimental group used creative visualization. The visualization consisted of resting quietly, usually before bedtime, and actively imagining a flawless performance on their next belt exam. Specifically, they were asked to create the sights, sounds, and smells associated with the exam, and also create a vision of themselves flawlessly performing kicks, forms, fighting, and so on. As expected, the experimental group performed better than either of the two other groups on the next exam.

Thinking about what the instructor has had to say that week in class is also important. It helps the student absorb and learn the "why" of the art, as well as the "how." This is critically important when the student is called upon to assist. One of my favorite American Zen epigrams comes from the late kempo pioneer Ed Parker, who said, "The student who knows *how* will always remain the student. The student who knows *why* will become the instructor."

To Assist and Return the Flow

Around fourth to third *kyu* or *gup* (brown belt), the instructor may call on the student to help with teaching, usually with the lower belts. As the student increases in rank, the responsibility of assisting the instructor and helping others as he has been helped becomes apparent. Students must attempt to pay back the instructor for all the time and effort that has been put into their own training. This is the concept of Karma, or "returning the flow." The teaching, knowledge, and wisdom that has flowed through the instructor and through the student, in turn, flows through to the other students. The interesting thing about returning the flow, however, is that by giving to others, the student actually gains in other ways. Some of the greatest insights I have had have come from teaching. The more you try to give, the more benefits come back to you.

To Show Respect

Along with assisting, students should give all due respect to the instructor. This not only sets the stage for others in the school to follow, but is an inherent part of the relationship. The student must have a high degree of respect for the instructor in order to be able to learn. This means both in the dojo in obvious ways (protocols) and outside the dojo in less obvious ways (by the student's behavior, which is a reflection on the instructor). Yes, the instructor must respect the students in their willingness to learn, but it is primarily the student's responsibility to respect and give deference to the instructor. When someone has the ability to make or literally break you, you'd better give that person every ounce of the respect that he or she deserves. If this is a problem, find another instructor you can respect. If you don't, you are cheating the (non-respected) instructor as well as yourself.

To Ask Questions Appropriately

Asking questions can be done appropriately or inappropriately. Inappropriately, it is done belligerently, with disrespect or animosity. Correctly, it becomes a quest for deeper understanding in order to become a more proficient martial artist or a more knowledgeable assistant. When done with humility and a genuine thirst for knowledge, students are able to reach a more thorough comprehension, thereby improving their martial arts skills and their ability to teach others. It may be, also, that the student has a question about why an instructor handles a situation either one way or the other. This generates the need for genuine communication, which is the final

and most important aspect of the instructor/student relationship.

The Mutual Responsibility: To Communicate

"When in doubt, talk it out" should be the motto here. In the old-school ways of thinking, this is unacceptable. Traditional Oriental and early American martial artists were taught—sometimes severely— not to question their sensei. They were to do as they were told, no more and no less. This probably worked very well in a society where life or death matters were an everyday occurrence. It's reminiscent of the militaristic notion that you never question a commanding officer. But does that work in today's environment in America? No way! Appropriate communication is the best way to keep the instructor/student relationship viable.

So much of what happens between people depends on the accurate interpretation of actions. For example, one of my favorite black belts had become increasingly withdrawn and unfriendly during and after class. My initial reaction was to not respond, thinking that something other than our relationship could be at issue. I even approached him once and he told me everything was okay. Then, after a period of time, I determined that the problem was not being resolved and action was needed. Finally, I was told that he had made several suggestions about things to teach in class that, for whatever reason, I had elected not to utilize. His interpretation of that was that I didn't value him as an assistant and that I was "dumping" him since he made black belt. Nothing could have been further from the truth. I just needed to let him know that it is inappropriate for a student to try to run a class unless asked to do so by the sensei. Once we both communicated, things got back on an even keel and the tension melted away. We were then able to relax and have fun again. When perceptions are different than what is intended, feelings are hurt and the relationship suffers as a result. If appropriate and honest communication takes place, however, explanations can be given and understanding is the result.

Understanding is composed of three basic elements: affinity, reality, and communication. Affinity is a primary liking of one another. This basis has to exist first, before the other two can come into play. Reality is a bit more complex, and has to do with expectations. As in the previous example, the reality for the student may be quite different from the reality held by the instructor. My student's reality was that he should be able to make suggestions about how to run the class, and that I would automatically try them. When that didn't meet my reality, his reality became that I had "dumped him" since he became a black belt. In my reality, that was ludi-

crous. Once we communicated about it, our realities became the same and understanding was again restored to the relationship.

Students should consider their responsibilities seriously and also be responsible and mature enough to communicate. Of course, the same goes for all you instructors out there—only more so! Only then will both instructor and student reap the inevitable and great rewards generated by genuine caring in the relationship between them.

This material originally appeared in the December 1995 issue of Inside Tae Kwon Do *magazine.*

32

Rank

How Easy Should We Make It?

Keith D. Yates

Tae Kwon Do instructor Jerry Racicot demonstrates a roundhouse kick.

When I started my martial arts training in 1965 there were only five belt colors in our system (the style Grand Master Jhoon Rhee, the "Father of American Tae Kwon Do," taught): white, green, blue, brown, and black.

I really can't remember when they added the orange belt, but I do remember why. It seems quite a few young students grew tired of waiting for that first colored belt and a lot of them were quitting. It seemed like a concession to impatience to me—after all, I had been a white belt for nine months. If it was good enough for us, it was good enough for them! But as I started teaching children as a brown belt, I came to realize that it probably was a good thing to set up a reasonable and achievable goal for kids. A few years later, Rhee introduced the gold belt (we called it a yellow belt). This was yet another, smaller step for the beginning students. The idea was to break the curriculum down into bite-sized pieces for the kids.

For that first belt, you only had to learn four basic blocks, along with a couple kicks and self-defense moves. In comparison, my first belt required six blocks, six kicks, punches, self-defense, three entire forms, and sparring. Remember, too, that it took almost a year to learn all of that. How would today's students respond to that amount of work and time at the beginning? Well, all they'd need to do would be to call the competition down the street and find out that they could make the first belt in four weeks or so. I wouldn't blame a parent for opting for the school that offers more frequent rewards.

Different Students, Different Systems

The big question here is does that approach—a quick colored belt—help or hurt the martial arts student in the long run? Are we caving in to society's penchant for instant gratification? Shouldn't the martial arts be about teaching patience and discipline?

One of my black belts teaches in a very traditional manner, in a university setting. He doesn't use the gold/yellow belt at all. He has very few examinations during the year and he has students—very good students—who have trained for six or seven years and still have a way to go until their first black belt test. He has fairly small classes and no children. He believes martial arts should be hard work and the goals should be such that, when achieved, you can be very proud of the accomplishment.

I have another student who runs a large commercial school. He has lots of kids in his classes and they have a great time. He plays games with them and has designed a curriculum with very few requirements at the beginning stages. He is more interested in keeping them having fun and staying motivated for the first few months, until they develop a love for the martial arts. His system has every col-

ored belt in the book and then some. He even has a "prebelt" stage for three-and four-year-olds with colored sashes denoting class attendance.

Which System Produces the Better Martial Artists?

Is the black belt who comes out of the very traditional setting—long hours of training for each belt—any better trained than the person who came up through a school with frequent promotions? In many cases, I have to admit the answer is yes. You have seen them at tournaments—the two-year black belts that were an embarrassment. They couldn't kick without losing their balance, their stances were terrible, they had no snap or power. How did they ever pass a black-belt test? Or, perhaps more to the point, what kind of black-belt test did they pass?

I truly believe there can be an acceptable compromise. We can find the proper balance. Teaching a lot of children, as I do in the YMCA, I acknowledge the advantages of small, achievable goals. In the "old days," most students didn't stick with Tae Kwon Do long enough to pass that first exam. Of the dozen or so people who started in my class of white belts, only two of us made it through the nine months to green. By comparison, I have had beginner classes with twenty-two white belts! They generally make it to yellow belt in a couple of months. Then we cover the material for orange stripe, then orange belt, then purple stripe, purple belt, green stripe, and, finally, green belt. By the time my students test for their green belt they have been taking lessons for nine months and know everything I had to for my 1965 green belt.

You know what the difference is? I'll probably have up to 90 percent of my students get that far, compared to the less than 10 percent of students my instructor promoted to green. So far, so good. But here's where the balance between old and new comes in. I begin to make the training harder by green belt.

Promotions take longer and the training becomes more intense. No longer will we give an "A for effort." The techniques must be performed correctly and powerfully. If you are not ready you don't get to test, and even if you do, you have no guarantee of passing. This is the way I make sure that my black belts of today are just as disciplined and skilled as the black belts of a generation ago.

Remember that student of mine who runs the commercial school with all the kids? He is one of only four black-belt instructors I have allowed to join our association who did not train with me since white belt. At first, I was wary of the many belts he uses. But as I observed his classes I realized that he had a proper balance between achievable goals and high standards. The thing I told him before he joined us was, "I don't really care how many belts you have as long as by the time your student gets to black belt, he or she really is a black belt."

It doesn't matter whose yellow belts have been training longer or whose are better, but it does matter whose black belts are better martial artists. You should be training with a school that knows the difference.

Keith D. Yates is president of the Southwest Tae Kwon Do Association (STA) and the founder of Nam Seo Kwan Tae Kwon Do. This material originally appeared in the January 1996 issue of Inside Tae Kwon Do *magazine.*

33

Thirty Things a Martial Artist Won't Tell You

Karen Eden

We've all seen the pictures. The ones where the karate expert looks "possessed," as if he's going to have an aneurysm—and that's just at the family barbecue! One can't help but wonder if he's not taking himself just a little too seriously.

Don't get me wrong, no one takes their martial arts training more seriously than I do, and though some traditionalists would disagree, there is a lot of humor in our industry, along with the discipline and respect. Just because Bruce Lee never smiled in his "pose downs" doesn't mean that he never smiled.

To the best of my knowledge, there's not a martial arts "bloopers" tape, but there sure should be. Someone yelling "oww!" after missing a board break, or someone turning the wrong way during a test, would make a great party tape to view while eating popcorn on the couch. As fellow karate comrades, we'd be lying if we didn't admit to making similar mistakes ourselves somewhere along our journey. The world needs to know that we didn't get this good "just like that." We messed up, we fell down, and at times we felt like real idiots out there before we finally got these ancient moves right. As an average, nonathletic person going in to sign up for private lessons, it sure would have been comforting to know that those black belts out there who made it all seem so easy were at one time just like me—a white belt who knew nothing more than what she was going to be taught. Yes, in spite of those pictures with the spine-chilling expressions, we're all just human beings, and learning to laugh at ourselves is the first step of great growth, and great humility.

Here's a list of things that a martial artist will never tell you. Should you find yourself chuckling as you read them, I, for one, promise that I will still respect you as a fellow martial artist.

- It's funny when you do a fisted-block with your middle finger in a cast.
- Your opponent is just as scared of you as you are of him.
- A black belt is confused because he's not allowed to beat you up, but he's also not allowed to let you beat him up.
- Why there's never any bathroom tissue at tournaments.
- Yes, that is dead skin on the floor.
- These uniforms sure are hot in the summer.
- It's humorous to watch the board-holders try to absorb the pain when someone misses the board.
- Just because you're a black belt doesn't mean that you can "part the Red Sea."
- Winning all of the time makes you feel pressured to win all of the time.
- The "horse-riding stance" looks really dumb in pictures.
- Regardless of your rank or your winning record, deep down you never feel like you're any good at this.
- They really thought of women when they designed these tops.
- If you want to be a good fighter, you have to learn how to relax.
- Accidentally hitting someone feels worse than getting hit.

- If the instructor looks down at the floor, he's trying to avoid laughing at you.
- "To be honest, I don't know how I won, I don't even remember what I did."
- There's always someone better, and there's always someone higher-ranked.
- Believe it or not, your instructor does wear street clothes.
- If someone asks you to take it easy on him, then he is going to pound you.
- Does it count if you hit a woman in the chest?
- "Does anybody want to take a break" is a trick question.
- Nothing hurts like you think it does.
- Why whenever you get hit, it's because you "walked right into it?"
- Every martial artist has bad days.
- You can't refer to your instructor as "my main man."
- Old people sure do hit hard!
- When in doubt, bow.
- Drawing blood does not mean you did good.
- The instructor is always right.
- "Please, cut your toenails."

Karen Eden is a Pittsburgh, Pennsylvania–based black belt and Tang Soo Do instructor and professional television broadcaster. This material originally appeared in the January 1996 issue of Inside Tae Kwon Do *magazine.*

34

Masters of What?

Guy Poos

Martial artists such as Jerry Racicot (left) know that true mastery comes from diligent practice that continues throughout one's life.

Thirty-five years ago, when I began my martial arts journey, I had but one expectation; I would learn the martial arts. I had no thought of rank, prestige, wealth, popularity, or importance.

You can see that I was very naive. From my simple understanding of what I thought the martial arts were, rank, wealth, and the like all belonged to the world of Western sport. The place where I was going was the pristine wilderness of internal harmony and Eastern serenity. I know what you may be thinking: Is this guy for real? I have to admit that I was in search of something that would last a lifetime and never be corrupt. I thought I had found the philosopher's stone in the martial arts.

In the early years of my training I began to have some doubts. I served a military tour of duty in Korea and experienced a different attitude toward the martial arts from the indigenous culture. I was somewhat confused, and a little dismayed. By the time I returned to the United States, the first wave of martial arts instructors was arriving. The ones with whom I came in contact were individuals with karate and Tae Kwon Do experience. One never knew how much experience they possessed, but even then, we Americans would always assume for the most part that they were dedicated practitioners and idealists cut from the same cloth from which legends are made. Once again, I was dismayed. But I cautioned myself not to be too quick to judge them.

It was then that I was introduced to the novel idea of the martial arts as an occupation from which to earn a living. Now, I was not completely naive; I knew some masters had traded martial arts expertise for some form of compensation. I was aware that instruction traditionally was bartered for any number of things, and after all, in the greatest market economy in the world, what would be more natural? Yet there was still something about this that did not seem quite right, and it quickly became obvious what that something was. It was the age-old dichotomy: Can you give payment for something that must be earned? The question remains: Did you buy it or did you earn it?

This problem now plagues the modern martial arts community. However, when all is said and done, this question is always answered in the character of the instructor. It follows that the most important element of the relationship between the instructor and the student has to be trust. You have to believe and trust the instructor that you have indeed earned your accomplishments and not simply bought them.

The Credentials of Early Pioneers

This brings me back to that first wave of karate and Tae Kwon Do instructors. We still do not know exactly what constituted their credentials. They have made this a moot point by now by either developing an honorable reputation, or becoming just another name associated with the shadowy history of American martial arts.

The thing that the early instructors in America all shared, however, is that they all had names rather than titles. Back then the highest accolade one could give them was teacher/instructor (*sensei*; *sabun nim*; *si fu*). If they had accepted an anglicized first name, we may even have called them by their first names.

Most of these individuals were making every possible attempt to identify with their adopted homeland. We could see their struggles and identify with their alienations and failures; they were human beings just like us. We also had opportunities to assess their physical qualifications. They would often train as part of their classes. Some, like W. Jack Hwang of Oklahoma and David Moon of Texas, even entered open tournaments and put their reputations on the line. Some who came from Korea continued to call their art "karate," even after the official naming of Korea's indigenous martial art as "Tae Kwon Do." Since their own training predated the reconstruction of Tae Kwon Do as a martial sport, they continued on the same familiar course they had originally charted. Some of them, in their Yellow Page ads, still refer to their martial arts instruction as karate.

Post-1973 Korean Tae Kwon Do Immigrants

This brings me to the waves of instructors who followed on the heels of the pioneers. I am addressing those with whom I have become most familiar, the Korean Tae Kwon Do "masters." This is the group that immigrated to the United States after the founding of the World Tae Kwon Do Federation in the early 1970s. This is also the group of instructors who introduced Americans to the exalted titles of "Master" and "Grand Master." Prior to their reemergence, these titles belonged to a misty time when old men and women, after dedicating their entire lives to martial arts training and instruction, had these titles bestowed upon them by grateful students and disciples. I cannot emphasize the word *training* enough.

They were not administrators, nor simply business-people looking for any way not to train and still make a buck. They were the real thing, practitioners of martial arts.

Is it possible that the definitions for master and grand master have changed over the last twenty or thirty years? If they have, it is about time we began recognizing this and judging these practitioners according to the standards that we impose on other mere mortals.

The Meaning of Mastership

We can approach mastership from at least two historical reference points, one Western and one Eastern. If we apply the Western view, we can then look at mastership as the quality of possessing superior technique, whether in the crafts or in the martial arts. You have a master weaver, journeyman weaver, and apprentice weaver. The apprentice is accepted by a master to be taught a craft until his service and skills warrant the title of journeyman. When he becomes a journeyman, he may begin working independently and earning a living as a member of the guild. We do not associate anything other than a skill level and, possibly, some instructional ability with mastership. In some cases the instructional ability may be nonexistent. The apprentice may simply learn through application.

If we apply the Eastern perspective, it involves some qualities and values that include elements of morality and social behavior in addition to technical mastery. It is here that the concept of the "cultivated person" in Chinese philosophy becomes appropriate. The "cultivated person" masters life by being well-rounded in all things and by displaying a morality that considers the welfare of all humankind individually and collectively, someone whose presence and behavior reflect the best that society has to offer. According to this definition, it would be impossible to be a master of life and engage in any of the common transgressions associated with many of the modern "masters" and "grand masters."

Tae Kwon Do pioneers such as Grand Master Jhoon Rhee have long recognized that being a "master" means being well rounded in all things and displaying a morality that considers the welfare of all human beings.

It is time for Americans to become more discerning and critical regarding mastership. I would find it difficult to credit mastership, by either the Western or Eastern definition, to someone who is very young, especially if there is little or no indication that he continually practices his art—or even enjoys it. I would be more likely to recognize a young person who had attained a simple technical proficiency as someone with a degree of mastership, than I would be to call such a person a master of life.

Personally, I find it inconceivable to give authority to someone whose basic values betray my understanding of what is good and right. Especially as Western students of the martial arts, we should reassess our own value systems. If we cannot do this, we should at least ask ourselves the question, what have these "masters" mastered?

Guy Poos of Edmond, Oklahoma, president of USA Taekwondo, has been involved in the martial arts for thirty-five years. This material originally appeared in the September 1995 issue of Inside Tae Kwon Do *magazine.*

35

Sticking With It
(When You Don't Know It's Working)

Karen Eden

If you feel different when standing in a crowd, then it's working. No one can put a price on the confidence and peace of mind you begin to feel even after just a few weeks of training.

The truth is, most of us will never star in a martial arts movie. Most of us won't win first place in a tournament, and most of us feel awkward and uncoordinated when we have to do a jump back wheel kick. The truth also is that most of us have regular jobs, and we hope that martial arts will be an asset to us both physically and mentally as we go about our daily routines.

If you occasionally feel like a big clumsy ox when practicing in class, that's okay. We all feel that way, especially when learning a technique for the first time. As a matter of fact, your instructor is doing his job by keeping things so challenging. The bottom line is that we all feel like we're not any good at times, and some days are better than others. But sometimes, it's just a matter of practicing. Some people catch on more quickly than others, some are more naturally athletic than others. Whatever your circumstances, you have to stick with it, even when you don't think it's working. Should you ever get discouraged about your training actually working for you, I encourage you to look at the big picture, and keep these things in mind:

1. *If you feel different when standing in a crowd, then it's working.* No one can put a price on the confidence and peace of mind you begin to feel even after just a few weeks of training. You walk differently, you stand differently, and you act differently. Just knowing that there's something different about yourself is proof that your training is working.

2. *If you can walk to your car at night and not be afraid, then it's working.* Believe it or not, after only a couple weeks of karate lessons, you've probably learned enough self-defense to save your life. It may not be pretty, but it will probably work for you. For the self-defense aspect alone, martial arts training is never wasted.

3. *If you can stand up to the temptations that try to master you, then it's working.* If you have enough courage to try to change your life, you've made a step in the right direction. The discipline and self-control which come from your martial arts training is what helps you do this.

Author Karen Eden (center) recognizes the spiritual benefits of staying with your martial arts training.

4. *If you can hold your peace after you've been insulted, then it's working.* There's something about knowing that you can seriously injure someone that makes you endure a lot more verbal abuse. There's something about being a martial artist that makes you feel less threatened, and less likely to believe the insults that may be hurled at you. Even though you know that you can physically conquer the average person, if you feel like it's totally unnecessary and unimportant to do so, then your training is working.

5. *If you find yourself searching for a deeper sense of spirituality, then it's working.* Those who think martial arts is about kicking and punching have quite an awakening coming to them. Martial arts will make you spiritual. When your mental state becomes heightened to the point where you want to be the very best person that you can be, and you start to feel more in balance with your physical self, you can't help but become spiritual. Martial arts has always dealt with spirituality as a way of becoming a more complete person.

Karen Eden is a Pittsburgh, Pennsylvania–based black belt and Tang Soo Do instructor and a professional television broadcaster. This material originally appeared in the June 1995 issue of Inside Tae Kwon Do *magazine.*

36

Hurry Up and Wait

Keith D. Yates

There is no "fast road" to success in martial arts.

Perhaps you've seen the cartoon of a guy standing in front of the microwave oven yelling, "Hurry up!" It's a funny cartoon because it is so true. We live in an age of instant gratification. From microwaves to fax machines, we are used to getting what we want "right now!"

Sure, it's nice to be able to see any movie you want any time you want on TV, and to be able to make a telephone call from anywhere on your cellular phone. But perhaps our reliance on all these gadgets affects our ability to be patient. For many people, the obsession with instant gratification has made them less tolerant when things don't go just right or when they take longer than expected. My dictionary defines "patience" as "the capacity or habit of bearing trials without complaint; not hasty or impetuous." It is the willingness to wait for the

185

desired results. What does this have to do with Tae Kwon Do? I'm glad you asked, Grasshopper!

One thing I constantly tell my younger students is, "No, you can't take the next belt test!" They will learn the training pattern for the next level and think they can immediately take the test. I tell them to be patient. Just because you memorized the steps doesn't mean you can perform the pattern with the proper balance, power, timing, and so on. You have to practice, sometimes for several months, before getting comfortable with the form. And this doesn't even address the topics of improving your self-defense, one-steps, and sparring skills—all of which take years to develop.

Of course, it's not only the kids who have to learn patience. Many times it is the adults that have been conditioned to expect immediate results. Like a farmer who plants seeds, you have to be willing to let nature take its course. You must water and wait and cultivate and wait and finally you can harvest. Sometimes the harvest isn't as good as you expected. As the farmer is willing to do it all over again the next season, you too must be willing to try to pass that test the next time or to do better in the next tournament.

Patience developed in the Tae Kwon Do classroom can influence your outlook on life in general. Many situations demand that after you have done everything possible, you must wait for the desired results. You can't always force things to happen. Life isn't like a microwave oven. You also sometimes have to learn to accept things the way they are. In spite of the fact that martial arts should teach you to be a person of action, there are still a few things that will be out of your control. Have the patience to realize that truth.

In some cases, impatience can cause you to take extreme actions that could actually produce the opposite results of those you want. Relax! Action taken in response to anxiety can be not only premature but unwise. An old Korean saying tells us, "It takes a year to harvest a crop, ten years to see the full beauty of a tree, and fifty years to make a man." Imagine the patience involved in a culture where the people are willing to wait fifty years before one is considered fully mature and wise. In American society, old citizens are put out to pasture. The baby boomers are past their prime. Generation "X" is where it's at. Perhaps we, as martial artists, can help reverse this trend toward instant gratification and help develop patience, beginning with our own lives.

Keith D. Yates is the president of the Southwest Tae Kwon Do Association (STA) and the founder of Nam Seo Kwan Tae Kwon Do. This material originally appeared in the June 1995 issue of Inside Tae Kwon Do *magazine.*

37

When Your Partner Has "Bad Control"

(The "Big Bull" Syndrome)

Karen Eden

There's One in Every Crowd!

There's at least one of them in every dojang. It doesn't matter how many speeches the instructor aims at him, the two words not in his vocabulary are "good control." Good luck to you if he's your sparring partner! On an easygoing day, maybe you can get away with a jammed finger. If he's feeling a bit aggressive, you'll wish you'd worn your cup and safety glasses.

Both men and women alike are guilty of having bad control. Some have no idea that they're even losing control or hitting too hard. Usually if you mention this to them, they'll apologize and calm down. There's nothing wrong with trying hard and wanting to do your best. We all take our turn at causing and being part of honest accidents. That's what protective

gear is for, and after all, we didn't sign up for golf lessons.

When Bad Gets Worse

However, there is a time when bad control gets out of hand, and that's when it is associated with a bad attitude. Some martial artists seem to have a need to be the "big bull." They insist on proving that they are the strongest, the bravest, and the toughest predators that the animal kingdom has ever seen. We'll call it the "big bull syndrome." Those who possess the big bull syndrome never give a female instructor respect. They often talk back and second guess her, feeling that no woman could possibly conquer them. Big bulls often become surrogate instructors to their fellow classmates, criticizing and teaching things that aren't their place to teach. And one final amazing aspect of big bulls is that deep down inside, they feel they can conquer their masters, and may someday rise to challenge them.

Reclaiming Control

From the beginning of time, there have been big bulls and big bull wannabes. Whether you're a partner with one, or are unfortunate enough to have one as a student in your class, here are some helpful tips to keep things under control, and bodily harm at a minimum:

1. *Team him up with a so-called "weaker" partner.* Someone who possesses such an attitude will not be threatened by children, or by women lower ranked than himself. By the same token, teaming him up with a higher-ranked student, or a larger male student, could result in a "locking of the horns."

2. *Try the yin and yang theory.* The Asians have known it for centuries. If he's fighting too aggressively, you become more passive. You calm down first, then he will calm down.

3. *Maintain your cool.* If the yin and yang theory doesn't work, you have every right to tell him to calm down. If he's higher ranked than you, keep your cool and talk with your instructor after class. Nobody should have to worry about going to work the next day hobbling or with a black eye.

4. *Think like an animal.* If someone is going to act like an animal, sometimes you need to think like an animal in return. A well-controlled, effective counterattack has been known to put a big bull in his place. I'm not saying to put him in traction, I'm just saying

to let him know who's really in charge. As animalistic as it may seem, it will usually work.

5. *Call a "meeting of the minds."* If an instructor is getting numerous complaints about a particular student, then it's time for the instructor and that student to have a serious talk. No instructor wants to lose students, but keeping one with an impossible attitude is a definite way of ruining your business and your reputation. Ask him to abide by the rules. If he can't respect you as an instructor by doing what you ask him to do, then he doesn't belong in your dojang. There are other schools that will readily take his business. Do yourself a favor and let them!

Karen Eden is a Pittsburgh, Pennsylvania–based black belt and Tang Soo Do instructor and a professional television broadcaster. This material originally appeared in the August 1995 issue of Inside Tae Kwon Do *magazine.*

38

When You Lose in Competition

Karen Eden

As top martial artists like Jerry Ellefson (left) know only too well, one must keep both life's joys and setbacks in proper perspective.

There couldn't be a worse feeling for the martial artist than the one you get the morning you wake up after a tournament, and you start to recall how badly you lost the night before.

The questions become increasingly annoying inside your head as you hit the shower: "Why didn't I punch more?" "They were kicking high to my head, why didn't I stay in closer?" Or, my favorite question, "Why did I just stand there?" As you head out the door for your next martial arts class, you start thinking up clever answers to that one question you dread having to answer to your classmates: "How did you do?" You could say, "Well I lost, but I had a really good time." Yeah, right. Or, "I got fourth place" (a good one for the family). But the best answer really is "I got my butt handed to me on a silver platter." Then laugh about it, and forget it.

Recover Your Perspective

Stop making excuses, and stop beating yourself over the head. It's just one tournament in a hundred that you could compete in if you wanted to, and if you do compete in a hundred tournaments, you'll eventually win something somewhere, because it's a numbers game half of the time anyway. Think about it. Someone getting lucky and scoring a couple of points in a two-minute period has nothing to do with what you could do to that person if he accosted you on the street. Point fighting is good for the soul, and a great way to see where you need to sharpen your skills, but it has very little to do with the real thing.

No one likes to lose, but there are normally only three winners per division, and sometimes that's going to exclude you. If you are a parent worried about the fairness of a tournament, then don't even put the kid in there, because many times tournament judging is not fair and there's no way to explain it. As long as your child understands this, then hand him his cup and mouthpiece and send him on his way; otherwise, spare him the agony of waiting around all day with very little food or water, just to come home empty-handed. Below are several ideas that may help you deal with the possibility of failure should you decide to compete again.

Never Plan on Winning

Using the power of positive thinking for something that relies on the opinion of someone else judging you is an automatic setup for failure. Just because you're good enough to win doesn't mean that you will win. If your instructor puts a lot of emphasis on bringing home a trophy or medal, I encourage you not to go. Bringing home a plastic and marble statue is not what martial arts competition is about. Having the courage to compete—risking not only your pride, but bodily harm as well—should be the only emphasis, along with earning the congratulations of your instructor.

Congratulate the Winners

Immediately after trophies have been given, go up and shake the hands of the winners. Congratulate them and feel the energy in their hands. Whether you think they should have won or not, try to share in their joy; after all, they couldn't have won without you being there. Sometimes seeing the joy in someone else's face will melt away the immediate feelings you have of envy, or of being a loser.

Keep Things in Proportion

When you lose, you may feel like the world is shining a huge spotlight on you, but the truth is, you're the one putting the spotlight on yourself. Nobody really cares, and they will soon forget that you lost, just as you forgot the hundreds of competitors who lost at the last tournament you were competing in. You may have heard it said, and it's true, that "Losing hurts more than winning feels good."

Make Your Energy Useful

It's the darndest thing, but when you take the time to help your junior belt classmates win, and they do win, you can't lose. They may take home the trophy, but in your heart, you have the trophy because they couldn't have won without you. Trust me, that can feel ten times as good as if you had won the trophy yourself.

Karen Eden is a Pittsburgh, Pennsylvania–based black belt and Tang Soo Do instructor and a professional television broadcaster. This material originally appeared in the March 1995 issue of Inside Tae Kwon Do *magazine.*

About the Editors

John Little's articles have been published in every major martial arts and health and fitness magazine in North America. He is considered the world's premier scholar on martial artist/philosopher Bruce Lee, having written more than fourteen books on Lee, his training methods, and his philosophy, including *The Warrior Within: The Philosophies of Bruce Lee* (NTC/Contemporary Publishing Group, Chicago), *The Tao of Gung Fu*, *The Art of Expressing the Human Body*, *Jeet Kune Do: Bruce Lee's Commentaries on the Martial Way*, and *Words of the Dragon* (Charles E. Tuttle, Boston). Little is the editor of the prestigious *Inside Kung-Fu* series (NTC/Contemporary) and *Bruce Lee: Words from a Master* (NTC/Contemporary), in addition to being the coauthor of *Power Factor Training*, *Static Contraction Training*, and *The Golfer's Two-Minute Workout* (NTC/Contemporary). Little received his B.A. in philosophy from McMaster University in Hamilton, Ontario, and spent his formative years in Agincourt and Muskoka. He is happily married and the proud father of four children.

Curtis Wong is the publisher of many of the world's leading martial arts magazines, including *Inside Karate*, *Inside Kung-Fu*, *Inside Kung-Fu Presents*, *Martial Arts Legends*, *Martial Arts Illustrated*, *Action Film*, *Paintball Games*, and the *Bruce Lee Quarterly*. He is the president of CFW Enterprises, a magazine and book publishing company in Burbank, California.